THE PACIFIC CENTURY

Study Guide

PUBLISHED IN COOPERATION WITH

The Pacific Basin Institute

IN CONJUNCTION WITH

The Annenberg/CPB Project

THE
PACIFIC
CENTURY
Study Guide

MARK BORTHWICK
AND **GIL LATZ**

with contributions by
Andrea Asbell, Blaine Erickson, and Paul Anton

Westview Press
BOULDER • SAN FRANCISCO • OXFORD

This book was developed for use with *The Pacific Century* college-level telecourse. The introductory Asian studies telecourse consists of ten one-hour public television programs, a text, this study guide, and a faculty manual. The series was produced by The Pacific Basin Institute in cooperation with KCTS-9/Seattle and NHK/Japan. Major funding was provided by The Annenberg/CPB Project. Additional funding comes from the Ford Foundation, the National Endowment for the Humanities, and the Henry M. Jackson Foundation. A generous contribution of published material was provided by The Asia Society and the East-West Center. *The Pacific Century* is closed captioned for the hearing impaired.

This Westview softcover edition is printed on acid-free paper and bound in library-quality, coated covers that carry the highest rating of the National Association of State Textbook Administrators, in consultation with the Association of American Publishers and the Book Manufacturers' Institute.

Published in 1992 in the United States of America by Westview Press, Inc., 5500 Central Avenue, Boulder, Colorado 80301-2847, and in the United Kingdom by Westview Press, 36 Lonsdale Road, Summertown, Oxford OX2 7EW

Library of Congress Cataloging-in-Publication Data
The Pacific century study guide / by Mark Borthwick
    p.   cm.
  Includes bibliographical references and index.
  ISBN 0-8133-1373-2
  1. East Asia—Politics and government. 2. Asia, Southeastern—
Politics and government—1945–   . I. Borthwick, Mark. II. Latz, Gil.
DS519.1.P273 1992
950—dc20   91-34127
                                                           CIP

Printed and bound in the United States of America

The paper used in this publication meets the requirements of the American National Standard for Permanence of Paper for Printed Library Materials Z39.48-1984.

10   9   8   7   6   5   4   3

Contents

iv

Acknowledgments

We would like to thank the Annenberg/CPB Project, whose support made this telecourse possible, and the Henry M. Jackson Foundation, whose grant to the Pacific Basin Institute supported the creation of the *Study Guide* materials.

For assistance developing the *Study Guide*, Beverly Collins, International Trade Institute at Portland State University, is recognized for her splendid work with page layout and final editing. Special appreciation is also extended to the Informational Graphics Laboratory, Department of Geography, University of Oregon, for its assistance in the preparation of maps found in the *Study Guide*. All maps were prepared from public domain files by David Cutting, cartographer.

Finally, we would like to thank Charles Scribner's Sons for permission to reprint excerpts from *Encyclopedia of Asian History*, Ainslie T. Embree, Robin J. Lewis, Richard W. Bulliet, Edward L. Farmer, Marius B. Jansen, David S. Lelyveld, and David K. Wyatt, eds. (New York: Charles Scribner's Sons, 1988), Copyright 1988 The Asia Society.

—Mark Borthwick
—Gil Latz

THE PACIFIC CENTURY:

Text Course and Telecourse

Study Guide Introduction

INTRODUCTION

The Pacific Century describes and explains the emergence, from the nineteenth century onward, of modern nations from the rich and varied cultures and societies of Pacific Asia. This introductory area studies telecourse provides students with an understanding of the historical and geographic context of the development of East Asia (China, Japan, Korea--and the Soviet Far East) and Southeast Asia (emphasizing Indonesia, Malaysia, the Philippines, Singapore, Thailand, and Vietnam).

The impact of early Western exploration and expansion are highlighted, but the larger scope of mutual transformation between East and West is also examined. We describe the accelerating pace of political, economic and cultural changes in a region whose economic output now rivals that of any other area of the world. As an epicenter of global commerce, Pacific Asia challenges us to better understand both the sources of its dynamism and the roots of its diversity.

Alongside the theme of modernization, *The Pacific Century* examines the persistence of tradition. In a region whose historic patterns of investing, trading, and voyaging now support a new age of commerce, it is essential to understand the cultural traditions and experiences that have formed today's contemporary Asian societies. Tradition and modernization often collided in the course of Asia's turbulent history, but in some instances their combination has also given rise to new expressions of parliamentary democracy and capitalism that neither the traditionalists nor the modernizers could have foreseen.

The geographic scope of *The Pacific Century* embraces the larger concept of the Pacific Basin. It has been from North America, principally the United States, that major energies and forces of change have emanated toward Asia. The interchanges with the United States are seen in this series to have enriched both sides of the Pacific Basin even as America, in the course of experiencing its own Pacific Century, has oscillated between isolationism and expansion, fear of subversion and confidence in success, support for stable authoritarianism and the advocacy of democratic change.

The Pacific Century telecourse makes comparisons and describes linkages, historical and cultural, within a very diverse geographical region. It challenges the student to use concepts from different disciplines such as anthropology, economics, geography, history, and political science to understand how the region has changed. In the end, it demonstrates that what awaits us in the next Pacific Century is best understood by studying the one that is now passing.

THE PACIFIC CENTURY: THE TELECOURSE

The Pacific Century provides a comprehensive look at the events and people shaping the last 150 years of Asia-Pacific history and relates them to the shape of Pacific Basin relationships today. It does so by integrating a ten-hour television series, *The Pacific Century*, sponsored by the Annenberg/CPB Project and the Ford Foundation, and a written text, *Pacific Century: The Emergence of Modern Pacific Asia*, by Mark Borthwick. The thirteen unit course consists of ten television and print units and three print-only units. The first week of the course, to be scheduled prior to the broadcast of the television programs, will introduce students to the geography and history of the Pacific Basin, and to major concepts of the course. Beginning with the second week of the course, reading and print study assignments correlate with the ten programs in the television series. Three additional course units, based on print-only materials, are available for special concentration on contemporary China, Indonesia, Vietnam, and the Soviet Far East. These extra units will be available for flexible use during or after the television broadcast.

In the following chart are descriptions of the thirteen *Pacific Century* units. Each description notes the video program and its relation to the text. When there is no film accompanying the textbook chapter, it is noted as a print-only unit. The linkages between the various units are also noted, for reference.

The Pacific Century:
Overview of the Relationship Between Written and Visual Materials

Unit	Unit Name, Assigned Chapters	Linkages	Television Program
1	Dynasties, Empires, and Ages of Commerce: Pacific Asia to the Nineteenth Century (ch. 1)	All Units	Print-Only Unit
2	The Seaborne Barbarians: Incursions by the West (ch. 2)	Unit 3	The Two Coasts of China: Asia and the Challenge of the West
3	Meiji: Japan in the Age of Imperialism (ch. 3)	Units 2, 7	The Meiji Revolution
4	The Rise of Nationalism and Communism (ch. 4)	Units 5, 11	From the Barrel of a Gun
5	Maelstrom: The Pacific War and Its Aftermath (ch. 5)	Units 4, 11	Writers and Revolutionaries
6	Post–WWII Asia: Reinventing Japan, Redividing Korea (pertinent sections: chs. 5, 6, 9)	Units 4, 5, 7, 10, 12	Reinventing Japan
7	Miracle by Design: The Postwar Resurgence of Japan (ch. 6)	Units 3, 6, 13	Inside Japan, Inc.
8	The New Asian Capitalists (ch. 7)	Units 7, 9, 13	Big Business and the Ghost of Confucius
9	Power, Authority, and the Advent of Democracy (ch. 8)	Units 8, 11	The Fight for Democracy
10	Sentimental Imperialists: America in Asia (ch. 9)	Units 5, 9, 12, 13	Sentimental Imperialists
11	China's Long March Toward Modernization (ch. 10)	Units 1, 5, 8	Print-Only Unit
12	Beyond the Revolution: Indonesia and Vietnam (ch. 11) and	Units 4, 5	Print-Only Unit
	Siberian Salient: Russia in Pacific Asia (ch. 12)	Units 2, 3, 10, 13	Print-Only Unit
13	Pacific Century: The Regional Perspective (ch. 13)	Units 6, 7, 10, 12	Pacific Century: The Future of the Pacific Basin

In order to take maximum advantage of the television programs, the student should ideally view them twice: the first time, to grasp the overall argument and concept of the program; the second time, to absorb its facts and evaluate specific issues and questions that it raises. More than one public television station may be available in the students' viewing area, so it is useful to look for alternate and repeat showings. Some schools will be able to offer video cassettes of the films.

THE PACIFIC CENTURY STUDY GUIDE

The purpose of the *Study Guide* is to aid students in their study of the material presented in *The Pacific Century*. Each Study Unit of this course takes a specific topical theme as its focus rather than providing a successive treatment of countries and cultures. The structure for examining these themes is as follows.

Each *Study Guide* unit consists of: an Overview, identification of Study Resources, Study Focus statements, a listing of Key Concepts and Names, a Glossary, Time-Frame Questions, Questions for Review, and Additional Recommended Readings.

Overviews: Condensed versions of the chapters, to reinforce the material covered.

Study Focus: Restatement of the ideas central to each unit and the course as a whole.

Key Concepts and Names: Identification of the key players, ideas, and places found in each chapter, specific elements the students should understand and remember.

The Glossary: Presentation of pertinent information about points, people, and places in the text, all in one concise entry. Pronunciation guidelines, dates, and summaries reinforce what the text covers; in some cases, Glossary entries give information not found in the text but helpful for a better understanding of material in the text.

Time-Frame Questions: Review of the significance and chronology of key events. Answers to all Time-Frame Questions are in the Answer Key, pages 163-164.

Questions for Review: Summary of the issues each chapter raises.

Additional Recommended Readings: List of books for further study, should the student be so inclined.

LARGER THEMES

In addition, several larger themes recur throughout this series that are intended to contribute to the overall coherence of *The Pacific Century*. They include the following:

"Progress" and Tradition: Economic development brings with it a sense of both gain and loss. Introduced notions of progress have challenged and altered cultural traditions that were, in any case, undergoing their own processes of change. The resulting tensions and demands on individuals and their societies have had a profound influence in the shaping of new Asian societies. Most important, leading Asian figures can be seen to have combined their own concepts of "culture" and "power" to create new nations.

Collisions between East and West: Ever since the first appearance of Western ships in Asian waters, the collision of cultures and ideas between East and West has been a dominant theme in the history of the Asia-Pacific region. We will examine the history of some of the more important Eastern and Western ideas and suggest how the interaction between them has influenced the history and contemporary shape of the region.

Democracy, Authority, and Power: Well before Eastern Europe launched its dramatic experiment with political liberalization, Asia-Pacific nations began to test the possibilities of democracy. In some cases, democracy withered in an environment of authoritarian control while in others it has advanced amid changing economic and cultural conditions. Often sacrificed to the demands of economic growth and stability, democracy has been defined to fit traditional attitudes about power and authority. *The Pacific Century* examines how such attitudes may be changing and what their impact has been on national development in different nations.

The United States in the Pacific: From its primarily commercial and cultural interests in the nineteenth century, the United States began an abrupt transition in its "Pacific" identity after acquiring the Philippines, suppressing a revolution by its people, and then, paradoxically, helping them to form an independent nation. *The Pacific Century* takes up the themes contained in this story to show how sentiment, fear, illusion, and benevolence have shaped the Asia-American relationship.

Economic Resources and Interdependence: Long before the advent of the European powers in the Pacific, Asians were engaged in commercial exchanges and dynamic international trade. The current economic boom in the region is an outgrowth of ancient patterns as well as an expanding global economy. Today, countries in the region face major challenges in making their growth equitable, stable, and healthy. Economic interdependence has also forced them to consider and begin to mobilize their common interests as a region in the global trading system.

DEVELOPING GEOGRAPHICAL PERSPECTIVES

A distinguishing characteristic of *The Pacific Century* is its attempt to introduce the student to the complex geography of the Pacific Asia region and the overarching concept of the Pacific Basin. This feature of the telecourse requires a word of explanation from the outset.

Numerous national studies highlight the fact that Americans in general, and students in particular, display alarming ignorance with regard to world regional geography. Thus, every effort is made throughout *The Pacific Century* to refer often and in detail to cartographic reference material or mapped data. This point is illustrated by discussion of regional geographical concepts, as found in the Introduction.

The challenge confronting the student is that of coming to terms with the geographical scale and diversity of Pacific Asia and the Pacific Basin. How is this to be accomplished? Identification of the geographical imperatives in the study of the greater Pacific region is an essential step toward answering this question.

Suggestions for developing an appreciation for the geographical diversity of the greater Pacific are several-fold. First, the student is encouraged to pay particular attention to the geographical themes contained in *The Pacific Century Study Guide*, that is, what is located where, and why. Second, in order to facilitate comprehension of the regions, countries, and places specified, three base and two thematic outline maps accompany the *Study Guide*, to be used for reference and for map exercise purposes. These maps can be found in the concluding pages of the Introduction to the *Study Guide*. Additional recommendations for their utilization can be found in the Study Focus and Questions for Review sections of the *Study Guide*. Third, the geographical perspective may be a novel way to look at this part of the world for some students; in those cases an important recommendation is to urge purchase of *Goode's World Atlas*, published annually by Rand McNally & Company, Chicago, Illinois. In paperback version, this comprehensive atlas is modestly priced for student purchase. It also has the added benefit of offering a complete *Goode's Atlas Study Guide* which includes review of: atlas usage; location of important places on the earth; and identification of the inter-relationships between people, places, and environments. Here one is exposed to such geographical concepts as <u>site</u> (absolute location), and <u>situation</u> (relative location: the external relations of a site to other areas), as well as other fundamental themes of geography. Atlas sections that depict Pacific Asia (e.g., Asia and its discrete regional subunits) as well as the Pacific Basin are clearly marked and matched to a set of base maps, also available from Rand McNally, which can be used for class exercise purposes.

Whether the student is new to regional study, or well versed, the objective of such cartographic analysis is to convey the diverse physical, cultural, political, and economic geography of Pacific Asia and the Pacific Basin. Selected phenomena worthy of comparative study include:

-confirmation of the location of all countries and major cities;
-confirmation of the area of all countries;
-confirmation of the population, population density, and population growth rate of all countries and major cities;
-confirmation of the location of major landforms, mountain ranges, and rivers in all countries;
-confirmation of the differences of climate, water resources, temperature, vegetation types, and soils in all countries;
-confirmation of the distribution of religion, ethnic groups, and types of agriculture in all countries; and
-confirmation of the distribution of levels of economic development (Gross National Product, Gross National Product per capita), size of military, and trading relationships (including mix of imports and exports) of all countries.

Data such as these capture the immensity, diversity, and complexity of Pacific Asia and the Pacific Basin. When presented cartographically, cogent generalizations about the characteristics of any given place or region become possible.

In summary, one of the important goals of *The Pacific Century Study Guide* is to develop a perspective from which Pacific Asia and the Pacific Basin may be better understood. A primary objective in this regard is identification of the component parts of, and interactions between, the Pacific rimland and basin countries. One effective way to encourage student acquisition of information about foreign areas and cultures is to emphasize the fundamental theme of geographic site and situation, as discussed above. Over the course of the thirteen study units

8

to follow, these two geographical constructs can be studied independently, or in tandem.

Particularly in the post–WWII period, the relationship between site and situation can serve to illustrate the apparent connectedness--or interdependence--of selected Pacific Asia and Pacific Basin countries. The basis of interdependence is the unequal distribution of resources, their conversion to finished products, and consumer demand. In this sense, resource location is the foundation of trade, underscoring the connections between the countries of the Pacific. Discussion of resource location, conversion, and final product consumption, through map exercises (and simple manipulation of statistical data), underscores the physical and organizational attributes of a site. Such knowledge promotes discussion of the factors contributing to economic and political development, including the distribution of wealth and poverty as well as ongoing transformation of a given society from rural to urban, and from agricultural to industrial. The progression from site characteristics to situational characteristics, as illustrated by trading patterns, confirms Pacific Basin interdependency.

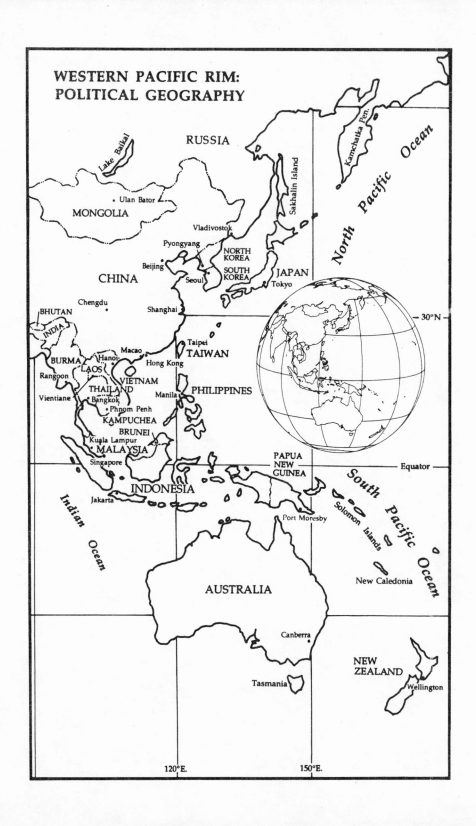

WESTERN PACIFIC RIM:
POLITICAL GEOGRAPHY

RUSSIA

Lake Baikal

Kamchatka Pen.

North Pacific Ocean

Sakhalin Island

• Ulan Bator

MONGOLIA

Vladivostok

Pyongyang

NORTH
KOREA

Beijing

CHINA

SOUTH
KOREA

Seoul

JAPAN

Tokyo

Chengdu

Shanghai

30°N

BHUTAN

INDIA

Macao

Taipei

TAIWAN

BURMA

Hanoi

Hong Kong

Rangoon

LAOS

VIETNAM

THAILAND

PHILIPPINES

Vientiane

Bangkok

Manila

• Phnom Penh

KAMPUCHEA

BRUNEI

Kuala Lampur

MALAYSIA

Singapore

PAPUA
NEW
GUINEA

Equator

INDONESIA

South Pacific Ocean

Jakarta

Indian Ocean

Port Moresby

Solomon Islands

New Caledonia

AUSTRALIA

Canberra

NEW
ZEALAND

Tasmania

Wellington

120°E.

150°E.

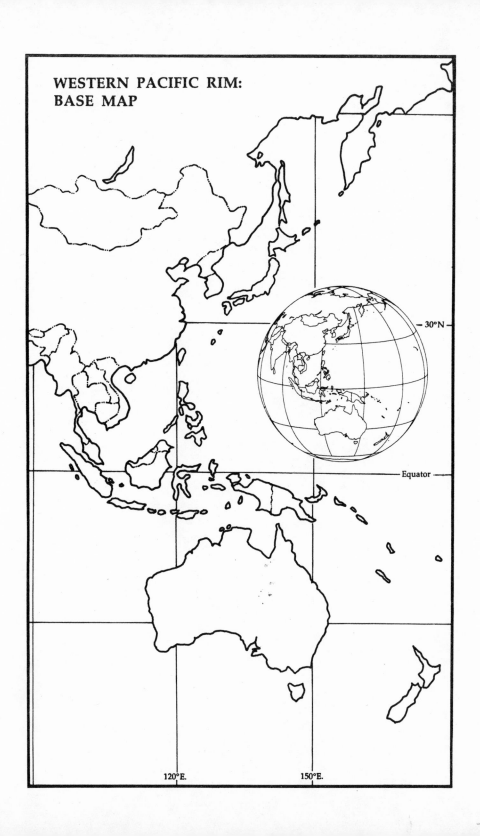

WESTERN PACIFIC RIM:
BASE MAP

30°N

Equator

120°E.   150°E.

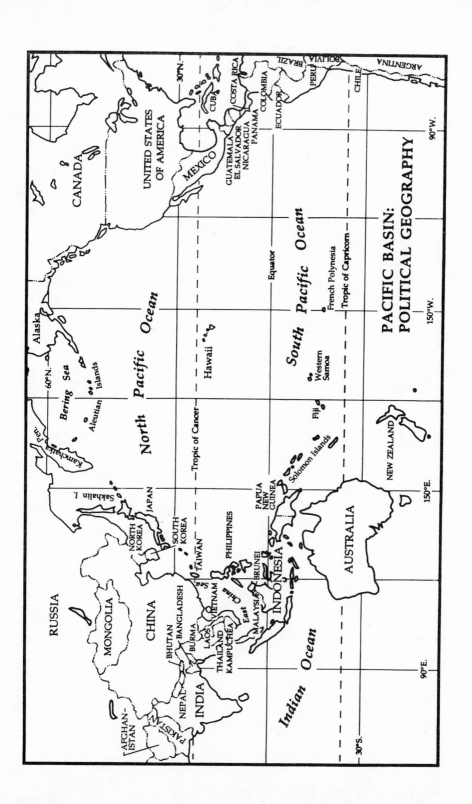

PACIFIC BASIN:
POLITICAL GEOGRAPHY

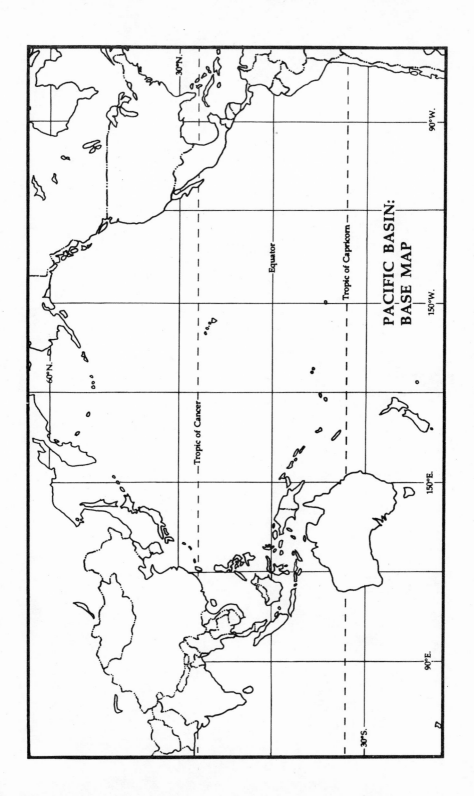

PACIFIC BASIN:
BASE MAP

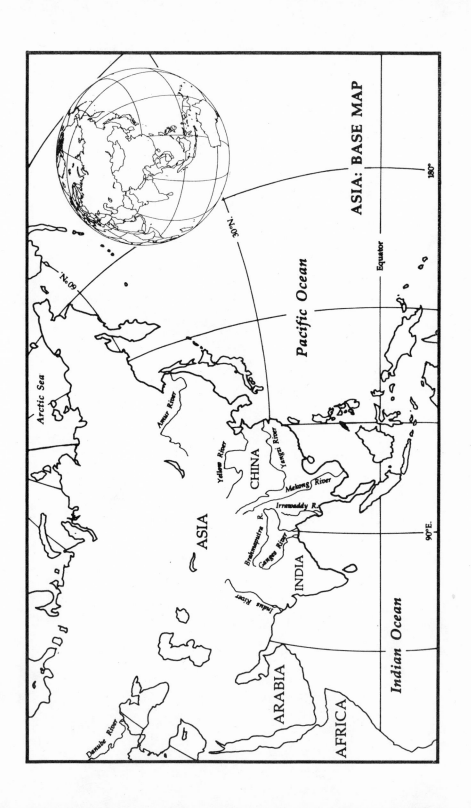

ASIA: BASE MAP

UNIT ONE

Dynasties, Empires, and Ages of Commerce:
Pacific Asia to the Nineteenth Century

OVERVIEW

The early civilizations of East and Southeast Asia, widely separated from one another, developed in distinctive ways that reflected their ethnic origins and physical surroundings. Beginning with the state of Qin, which established key precedents for the first and all future dynasties in China, the geographical scope and military power of China expanded greatly. Its bureaucratic organization grew stronger; Chinese language spread in usage; and Confucianism, along with other philosophies, gained in prominence and influence. With the advent of the Tang Dynasty (618 CE), China came to exert a powerful influence, politically and culturally, throughout East Asia. Contact with the distant Mediterranean world was modest but influential over the following centuries, fluctuating according to the openness of the Silk Road and maritime routes.

Elsewhere in Pacific Asia, evidence about the patterns of commercial life, political development, and culture appears somewhat later, but the distinctiveness of the various traditions is clear at a very early stage. Koreans contended with one another and with invasions from China and the north. Japan, geographically less vulnerable, was influenced culturally from the mainland and soon developed in the direction of a competitive, feudalistic system.

In Southeast Asia, the maritime trading empire of Srivijaya, built on the dynamics of intra-regional trade and the flow of goods between China and India, dominated the local seas from the eighth to the twelfth centuries CE. Great Kingdoms such a Angkor rose on the mainland and, like counterparts in the island regions, it battled with rival kingdoms for prominence and territory.

Migratory movements and outside cultural influences combined with indigenous traditions to both alter and complicate the mosaic of peoples in Southeast Asia. The impact of Indian and Moslem influences has been especially profound, but in the fifteenth century the arrival of an expeditionary fleet from China set the stage for a new period of international commercial expansion. This flourishing world of

Southeast Asian commerce was to be supplanted by European intruders in the following centuries, but while it lasted it reflected a growing wealth and prosperity in an international community stretching from the Levant to the China coast.

Pacific Asia was *not* a static and unchanging world when the Europeans began arriving in larger numbers in the sixteenth century. During Europe's medieval period, Pacific Asia could boast several cities of greater size and wealth. The average standard of living and scale of commerce in China was probably well above that in Europe.

STUDY RESOURCES

Text: Chapter 1: *Dynasties, Empires, and Ages of Commerce: Pacific Asia to the Nineteenth Century*

STUDY FOCUS

After reading Chapter 1, you should have a basic understanding of the following concepts.

1. China and Chinese culture had great influence on Korea, Japan, and Vietnam. Confucianism and written Chinese were two important parts of this cultural influence.

2. Buddhism, albeit in different forms, spread into East and Southeast Asia. It remains a significant religious tradition in the Asia Pacific region.

3. Hinduism and Sanskrit were two important elements of Indian culture that were borrowed and adapted by the peoples of Southeast Asia.

4. Islam spread into much of Island Southeast Asia, beginning in the sixteenth century, often displacing the religions that had been there before.

5. Regardless of the enormous impact of cultural borrowings throughout East and Southeast Asia, each region and each nation remained culturally distinct.

6. Southeast Asia and East Asia can be differentiated in terms of their location, physical environment, and cultural characteristics. This is true both historically and in the contemporary period, even if the

juncture of the two regions presents some ambiguities, as exemplified by Vietnam.

KEY CONCEPTS AND NAMES

This is a list of important terms, people, and places that you should understand from reading the text. If you cannot think of a brief definition for all of these words, you need to read the text again.

Angkor	Qin Shihuangdi
Buddhism	Samurai
Confucius	Shinto
Dao/Daoism	Shogun
Han Dynasty	Silk Road
Indianization	Silla
Islam	Srivijaya
Khmer	Tang Dynasty
Koryo	Vietnam
Legalism	Yangzi River
Mandate of Heaven	Yi Dynasty
Mongol Empire	

GLOSSARY

Note on pronunciation guidelines: Many Glossary entries have pronunciation guides. These appear, in parentheses, at the beginning of an entry. Whenever possible, English words have been used; they should be pronounced as they would in English. For details on the pronunciation of a given language, please see the text.

■ General

BCE/CE: Acronyms for Before Common Era and Common Era. A system of dating which corresponds exactly with the Christian calendar. Unlike the Christian dating system, both BCE and CE come after the year.

Examination System: A method of selecting civil servants by testing knowledge of the Chinese classics. It was employed in China (its country of origin), Korea, and Vietnam.

Kublai Khan: 1215-1294. Grandson of Genghis, Kublai became the Great Khan in 1260. Under his rule, the Mongol empire became the largest land empire ever formed.

Mahayana: (ma ha yah nah) Literally, "Greater Vehicle," implying it is the superior way to propagate Buddha's message. Mahayana Buddhism spread into China, Korea, Japan, Vietnam, and part of Southeast Asia. It emphasizes salvation through congregations, erection of temples, use of holy imagery, and chanting of short prayers.

Siddhartha Gautama: (sid heart tah gow ta ma) Circa 560-480 BCE. The name of the Indian prince who achieved enlightenment and became known as Buddha ("enlightened one").

Silk Road: From German *Seidenstrassen* ("silk roads"). The Central Asian trade routes which linked Asia and Europe. Trade along the Silk Road began during Han times; its peak was during the Tang dynasty. Art, philosophy, religion, and technology also travelled the Silk Road. Though individuals rarely travelled more than a short part of the route, goods went as far as Japan in the east and Britain in the west.

Son of Heaven: Derived from the Chinese term *Tianzi*, it is a traditional term for the Chinese emperor. The Vietnamese also used this term for their emperors, but it was never used in Japan.

Sutra: Buddhist holy text.

Theravada: (tare ah vah dah) The form of Buddhism prevalent in Burma, Cambodia, Laos, Sri Lanka, and Thailand. Older and more conservative than Mahayana, Theravada emphasizes individual effort towards salvation, particularly by becoming a monk or nun. Also known as Hinayana ("Lesser Vehicle"), although Theravada is just one sect of Hinayana Buddhism.

Yalu River: Chinese for Amnok-kang, the 790 km-long river which forms the boundary between Manchuria and northern Korea.

■ **China**

Chinese Dynasties: Note: Some of these dates are approximate.

Qin	221 BCE-206 BCE	Tang	618-907
Han	206 BCE-220 CE	Song	960-1279
Three Kingdoms	220-280	Yuan (Mongol)	1280-1368
Six Dynasties	222-589	Ming	1368-1644
Sui	581-618	Qing (Manchu)	1644-1912

Beijing: (bay jing) Literally, "northern capital." First used by the Mongols as their capital, the Ming also used Beijing as their administrative center. Beijing was the Qing capital, and is the capital of the People's Republic of China (PRC).

Daodejing: (dow duh jing) Also known as Tao-te Ching. Literally, "Classic of the Way and its Virtue." Traditionally ascribed to Laozi, this brief work ranges from poetry to philosophy to mysticism and has inspired more commentaries and translations than any other classical Chinese work.

De: (duh) "Virtue." That which an emperor possessed when he also had the Mandate of Heaven.

Eunuch: A castrated man. Eunuchs, who served as guards, were the only men other than the Emperor allowed to reside in the imperial palace.

Han Chinese: (hahn) A term of ethnicity used for the "Chinese" people of China, as opposed to any of the non-Chinese peoples (e.g., Mongols, Manchus). Identity as "Han Chinese" came from the Han dynasty.

Han Dynasty: 206 BCE-221 CE. The second dynasty of unified China and the first great Chinese empire. The Han continued what the Qin had started, in that the Han brought more area under imperial rule, further consolidated the pattern of central power, and set precedents that were followed for 2000 years.

Jurchen: The name of a tribe of the Manchurian plain. In 1115, the Jurchen founded the Jin dynasty in northern China. The Jurchen defeated the Northern Song in 1127. The Jin dynasty, also called the Ruzhen (roo juhn) dynasty, lasted until 1234, when the Mongols conquered it.

Laozi: (lao tsuh) Traditionally considered to be the author of the *Daodejing*, and to be the founder of Daoism. There is no consensus as to when he lived or even if he lived, but he is placed anywhere from 600 to 200 BCE. Laozi may be no more than a legendary figure drawn from the lives of several early philosophers.

Legalism: A Chinese school of thought which assumed human nature to be basically evil; humans had no inborn moral goodness. Reward and fear of punishment were central to governance. Legalist government was based on impartial law, rather than moral virtue. Qin Shihuangdi and Li Si were two prominent Legalists.

Loess: A fine grained, silt-like material, generally thought to have been deposited by wind. Concentrated in northwest China, particularly

Shaanxi province. Where vegetation has been removed, loesslands can be severely eroded into a highly dissected landscape resembling badlands. Loess soils are also found in America and Europe. The Yellow River gets its name from the great amount of loess it carries.

Middle Kingdom: Traditional literal translation of the Chinese term for China (*Zhongguo*). It implies that China is central to the world order, existing between heaven and the rest of the world.

Nanyang: (nahn yahng) Literally "south seas," it refers to areas south of China. *Nanyang* also refers to overseas Chinese.

Qin Shihuangdi: (chin sure hwong dee) 258 BCE-210 BCE. Given name Zheng (juhng). After ascending to the Qin throne, King Zheng extended his rule to include the other kingdoms of China, and proclaimed himself emperor over all. His dynasty did not last long after his death, but his influence on China is felt to this day.

Song Dynasty: (soong) 960-1279. The Song dynasty reached great artistic and intellectual heights. (Neo-Confucianism was developed during Song times.) Domestic trade also advanced under the Song.

Tang Dynasty: (tahng) 618-907. The second great Chinese empire, Tang China was the most civilized and developed country on earth at its height. Tang China reached pinnacles in art, literature, and music; the Tang capital, Chang'an, was a cosmopolitan city with traders from faraway lands, all of whom brought their own religions, customs, and food. Tang China reached its peak in size in the 660s, when it spread from the East China Sea to Persia. Internal dissent in the eighth century led to the eventual fall of the empire.

Xi'an: City in western China, on the site of the capital of the Qin, Han, and Tang dynasties. Its old name was Chang'an--"everlasting peace."

Yellow River: Mandarin, Huang He. A river that flows through north central China; it is the traditional cradle of Chinese civilization. Known as "China's Sorrow," because of its frequent and devastating floods. Called the Yellow River because it carries the infamous yellow loess soils of northern China.

Yuan Dynasty: (you ahn) 1280-1368. The dynasty founded by the Mongols.

Zhong Ke: (jong kuh) Would-be assassin of King Zheng of Qin (Qin Shihuangdi)

■ <u>Japan</u>

Ashikaga: (ah she caw gah) The family name of the Shoguns of the Muromachi *bakufu*, who ruled from 1338 to 1573. See Chapter 3.

Bushido: (boo she doe) Literally, "Way of the Warrior." Central to *Bushido* are complete loyalty to one's master and readiness for death in an instant. *Bushido* evolved from a warrior ethic present since Kamakura times, and was influenced by Zen and Confucianism.

Fudai: (foo dye) The hereditary vassals of the Tokugawa clan. Also used to describe those factions friendly to the Tokugawa before the Battle of Sekigahara.

Fujiwara: (foo gee wa raw) The name of an aristocratic clan that had enormous influence during the Heian period.

Heian: (hay on) The name of a period (794-1185). During this period, courtiers controlled Japan from palaces in Kyoto, while living a life of luxury. This period saw great development in Japanese architecture, ceramics, literature, painting, sculpture, and textiles. Buddhism also gained greater influence; several new schools of Buddhist thought were introduced from China.

Kamakura: (caw ma coo raw) Once the seat of the Minamoto shogunate, Kamakura is a mid-sized city on the Pacific Ocean, close to Tokyo. Kamakura is also the name for the era of Minamoto rule (1192-1333).

Kamikaze: Literally, "divine wind." Great storms devastated the invading fleets of the Mongols in 1274 and 1281, saving the Japanese from further fighting. It was thought that Japan received divine protection, and this was manifestation of that favor.

Kokugaku: (co coo gah coo) "National Learning." A school of thought developed during the Edo period. It emphasized Japanese traditions over Chinese scholarship and recent Western studies (*rangaku*).

Kyoto: (kyo toe) The capital of Japan from 794 to 1868. The Japanese capital is where the emperor lives, and was not always the seat of government. Heiankyo ("Peaceful Capital") was its name during the Heian period.

Minamoto: (me nah mow toe) The name of the samurai clan that achieved supremacy in the late twelfth century. The Minamoto ruled Japan from Kamakura from 1192 to 1333.

Muromachi: (moo roe ma chee) The seat of the Ashikaga shogunate, Muromachi is the name of a section of Kyoto. Muromachi is also a name for the period of Ashikaga rule (1338-1573).

Nara: The first permanent capital of Japan; also the name of the period when the city served as the capital (710-784). Heijokyo ("Peaceful Castle Capital") is the ancient name for Nara.

Oda Nobunaga: (oh dah no boo nah gah) 1534-1582. One of three great generals of the sixteenth century, he brought most of Japan under his rule. However, before he could unify the nation, he was assassinated.

Rangaku: (rahn gah coo) Literally, "Dutch Learning." The study of Western medicine, science, and technology during the Edo period; it can also mean study of the Dutch language. As the Dutch were the only traders with a permanent enclave in Japan during Tokugawa times, they were the sole conduit for Western learning.

Samurai: The hereditary military/ruling class of Japan.

Shinto: Indigenous religion of Japan. Shinto is more a collection of folk beliefs and rituals than a codified religion. Central to Shinto are *kami*, often translated as "god" but perhaps better rendered as "spirit". *Kami* are as diverse as mountain spirits, tree spirits, rock spirits, natural phenomena (such as wind and thunder), and even famous people. There is great regional variation in Shinto practice, and the rites focus on purity, beauty, and harmony.

Shogun: The military governor of Japan. Minamoto Yoritomo was the first to claim this title. Subsequent Shoguns were also of the Minamoto clan, although their family names were different (Ashikaga, Tokugawa). *Bakufu* is the Japanese term for "shogunate."

Taika Reforms: (tie caw) *Taika*, literally "Great Change," was a governmental reform carried out in 645. The government was based on Tang models; Buddhism was the state religion. Government based on the Taika Reforms lasted through the Heian period.

Tokugawa: (toe coo gah wah) The name of the clan that ruled Japan from 1603 to 1867. This period is called the Tokugawa period; it is also known as the Edo period.

Tokugawa Ieyasu: (ee eh yah sue) 1542-1616. A master strategist in his own right, Ieyasu built upon Hideyoshi's work to bring Japan under his rule. His decisive victory at Sekigahara in 1600 brought all Japan under his rule; he became Shogun in 1603.

Toyotomi Hideyoshi: (toe yo toe me he deh yo she) 1536-1598. Hideyoshi rose from a humble background to become ruler of all Japan. A brilliant strategist and general, Hideyoshi was a lavish patron of the arts and an innovative ruler. Often called a megalomaniac, Hideyoshi envisioned Japanese rule over China. Twice, Hideyoshi ordered the invasion of Korea; he died during the second invasion, which was then called off.

Wa: Ancient Chinese term for Japan.

Yamato: (yah ma toe) A term used to refer to Japan, Japanese things, and the Japanese people. *Yamato* is also the ancient name for the Nara area, and the name of a historical era (circa 300 to 710).

Zen: A sect of Buddhism which became popular in Japan after two great monks, Eisai (1141-1215) and Dogen (1200-1253), made pilgrimages to China. Zen emphasizes individual meditation (*zazen*) as the means to attain enlightenment. Zen, popular among the samurai, profoundly influenced Japanese art and is the basis for Bushido. Zen is called *Chan* in Mandarin and *Son* in Korean.

■ Korea

Hangul: (hahn ghoul) Promoted by King Sejong (r. 1418-1450), *hangul* is a phonetic alphabet used to write Korean.

Hwarang: "Flower youths." An elite corps of troops formed by Silla, the *hwarang* were trained in both literary and martial arts. Their philosophy was based on Buddhist and Confucian values.

Koguryo: (co goo ryo) One of Korea's three ancient kingdoms, Koguryo ruled the northern two-thirds of Korea from 313 to 668. Buddhism entered Koguryo in 372. In 668, the combined Silla and Tang armies defeated Koguryo.

Koryo: (co ryo) Founded in 918, Koryo controlled the entire Korean peninsula by 935. The word "Korea" is derived from Koryo. Buddhism and Confucianism flourished under the Koryo kingdom. The government was Confucian-based and was greatly influenced by Song China.

Koryo was invaded by the Mongols in 1231, and lost its autonomy to the Mongols in 1273. In 1392, General Yi Song-gye turned against Koryo and toppled it.

Paekche: (pak cheh) One of Korea's three ancient kingdoms. Founded in 350, Paekche controlled the southwestern quarter of the Korean peninsula, and was the conduit for the flow of Chinese culture to Japan. In 663, Paekche fell to Silla.

Silla: One of Korea's three ancient kingdoms, Silla controlled the southeastern third of Korea from 356. After conquering its rival states in the 660s, Silla ruled the Korean peninsula until 935, when it was overcome by Koryo. Silla reached great artistic heights, and much of Korea's traditional culture is based on Silla's achievements.

Sirhak: "Practical Learning." A school of thought that emphasized Korean culture and identity over pervasive Chinese influence. It also stressed practical application, such as agriculture, defense, and trade.

Sowon: Private Confucian academies, located in areas outside of major Korean cities. *Sowon* represented different groups of *yangban* and added to the factionalism of Yi Korea. *Sowon* were endowed with their own lands, which were removed from the imperial tax registers.

Turtle Ships: Ironclad boats with plated decks; the plating was rounded and resembled a turtle's shell. Admiral Yi Sun-sin, commanding a fleet of turtle ships, successfully defended against the Hideyoshi-ordered Japanese invasion of Korea.

Yangban: (yahng bon) The educated aristocracy of Korea.

Yi Dynasty: Also known as the Choson ("Morning Serenity") Dynasty. In 1392, while leading an expedition against the Ming, General Yi Song-gye, a Koryo general, turned against Koryo and toppled it. One of the Yi kings, Sejong, brought about a golden age in Korean history.

   The Manchus invaded Korea in 1627 and 1636, and forced the Yi court to acknowledge Manchu supremacy. The Yi ruled Korea until 1910, when Japan annexed Korea.

■ Southeast Asia

Angkor: A state of mainland Southeast Asia, usually given the dates 802 to 1432. Founded in the area north of Lake Tonle Sap in Cambodia, Angkor eventually spread its rule over much of modern Cambodia, Laos, Thailand, and Vietnam. Angkor's power was based on its ability to maintain and regulate reservoirs, which allowed it to grow three crops per year and made possible a large population. Although there is no consensus as to why Angkor fell, wars with rival states certainly exacerbated Angkor's weakness, contributing to its fall.

Annam: "Pacified south." A demeaning Chinese term for Vietnam.

Brahmin: The highest Hindu caste. Brahmins often become priests. Although a caste system was not adopted in Southeast Asia, priests in Southeast Asia were called Brahmins. Brahmin is also spelled Brahman.

Chakri Dynasty: The royal house of Thailand. The first Chakri king, Rama I, ascended the throne in 1782. Bhumibol Adulyadej, enthroned as Rama IX, is the present king of Thailand.

Champa: A state which existed along the coast of Vietnam from the sixth to the fifteenth century. The people of Champa are called Chams.

Khmer: Term for the language and people of Cambodia.

Malacca: Also spelled Melaka, Mulucca. A port city and entrepôt on the west coast of peninsular Malaysia, Malacca is also the name for the strait dividing Sumatra and peninsular Malaysia.

Malay: A term of ethnicity, used for one of the peoples of Southeast Asia. Malay also refers to the language of Brunei, Malaysia and Indonesia.

In the Malaysian constitution, a Malay is defined as one who follows Malay customs, speaks Malay, and professes Islam.

Nanyang: A Chinese term for Southeast Asia, meaning "the southern region."

Siam: Old term for Thailand.

Southeast Asia: A term used to designate the area encompassing modern-day Brunei, Burma, Cambodia, Indonesia, Laos, Malaysia, Philippines, Singapore, Thailand, and Vietnam.

Srivijaya: (sree vee jaw yah) A maritime trading empire that existed on peninsular Malaysia and Sumatra from the seventh through fourteenth centuries. Srivijaya, a tributary state of China, acted as a conduit for trade between China on the east and India and Persia on the west. Srivijaya ruled both sides of the Malacca Strait, and was able to control traffic within the strait. In 1025, forces from India attacked Malacca, smashing its authority in the strait; Srivijaya never fully recovered from this attack.

Wat: (watt) Southeast Asian term for Buddhist temple.

TIME-FRAME QUESTIONS

Place the items in each question in the proper chronological order.

1. a. Qin dynasty
   b. Tang dynasty
   c. Qing dynasty
   d. Han dynasty
   e. Three dynasties

2. a. Beginning of trade on the Silk Road
   b. Murasaki Shikibu writes *The Tale of Genji*
   c. Buddhism reaches China
   d. Promulgation of *hangul* by King Sejong
   e. *Analects* compiled

3. a. Rise of Srivijaya
   b. Chinese envoy Zhou Daguan visits Angkor
   c. Matchlock rifle introduced to Japan
   d. Vietnam gains independence from China
   e. Magnetic compass used by Chinese

4. a. Tokugawa Ieyasu
   b. Murasaki Shikibu
   c. Shotoku Taishi
   d. Minamoto Yoritomo
   e. Oda Nobunaga

5. a. Yi dynasty founded
   b. Silla unifies Korea
   c. Han colonies (Lelang)
   d. Hideyoshi invades Korea
   e. Koryo founded

6. a. Song dynasty
   b. Six Dynasties
   c. Sui dynasty
   d. Yuan dynasty
   e. Ming dynasty

7. a. Fall of Paekche
   b. Fall of Angkor
   c. Fall of Tang dynasty
   d. Fall of Kamakura shogunate
   e. Fall of Ashikaga shogunate

8. a. King Sejong
   b. Yi Song-gye
   c. Choe Chung-hon
   d. Wiman
   e. Yi Sun-sin

9. a. Rise of Angkor
   b. Fall of Srivijaya
   c. Spread of Indian influence in Southeast Asia
   d. Rise of Thai kingdom
   e. Rise of Java

10. a. Han Wudi
    b. Confucius
    c. Ming Hongwu
    d. Marco Polo
    e. Ghengis Khan

QUESTIONS FOR REVIEW

1. Look at the list of Key Concepts and Names for this chapter. Find all the place names, then locate each place on the maps in the text. Also, look for the following rivers: Mekong, Red, Yalu, Yangzi (Yangtze), Yellow (Huang).

2. What are unifying forces in East Asia? in Southeast Asia? Which forces go beyond national boundaries and serve to culturally unify vast areas? Why?

3. What effect did the intellectualism of Confucianism have on China? To what other countries did Confucianism spread? Did it have the same effect in these countries as it had in China?

4. Factionalism is an identifying feature of both Korean and Japanese political processes; indeed, factionalism remains important in modern Korean and Japanese politics. How much of a role has factionalism played in China?

5. What were some of the effects of Indianization on Southeast Asia? How did Indian cultural influences interact with indigenous traditions? How did India affect language, religion, and culture?

6. What features identify Vietnam with the rest of Southeast Asia? What features set it apart? Why?

7.   What are some of the differences between unifying and ruling Japan or Korea versus unifying and ruling China? Think about the countries' sizes.

8.   What was the most important factor in Angkor's rise to power? How did the Khmers capitalize on their power? What brought Angkorian rule to an end?

9.   Chinese influence spread widely. Name the areas to which it spread, and the features adopted (and adapted) in each area. What features of Chinese civilization remained exclusively Chinese (i.e., were not adopted)? How did indigenous cultural features change under the Chinese influence? How did Chinese culture change in new environments? Be specific.

10. Srivijaya was a major traditional culture in Southeast Asia. What were the factors in Srivijaya's rise? What were the pressures that contributed to Srivijaya's fall?

ADDITIONAL RECOMMENDED READINGS

Bong-Youn Choy. *Korea: A History*. Rutland, VT & Tokyo: Charles E. Tuttle Company, Inc., 1982.

Bownas, Geoffrey and Anthony Thwaite, trans. *The Penguin Book of Japanese Verse*. New York: Penguin Books Ltd., 1983.

Carpenter, Frances. *Tales of a Korean Grandmother*. Rutland, VT & Tokyo: Charles E. Tuttle Company, Inc., 1973.

Hall, John Whitney. *Japan: From Prehistory to Modern Times*. Rutland, VT & Tokyo: Charles E. Tuttle Company, Inc., 1985.

Lao Tsu. *Tao Te Ching*. Trans. Gia-Fu Feng and Jane English. New York: Vintage Books, 1972.

Lee, Peter H. *Anthology of Korean Literature From Early Times to the Nineteenth Century*. Honolulu: University of Hawaii Press, 1981.

Merson, John. *The Genius That Was China: East and West in the Making of the Modern World*. Woodstock, NY: Overlook Press, 1990.

Meskill, John T. *An Introduction to Chinese Civilization*. Lexington, MA: D.C. Heath and Company, 1973.

National Geographic Society. *People and Places of the Past: The National Geographic Illustrated Cultural Atlas of the Ancient World*. Washington, DC: National Geographic Society, 1983.

Osborne, Milton. *Southeast Asia*. Sydney: George Allen & Unwin, Ltd., 1985.

Reid, Anthony. *Southeast Asia in the Age of Commerce 1450-1680: The Lands Below the Winds*. Vol. 1. New Haven, CT: Yale University Press, 1988.

Sansom, G.B. *Japan: A Short Cultural History*. Rutland, VT & Tokyo: Charles E. Tuttle Company, Inc., 1986.

Schirokauer, Conrad. *A Brief History of Chinese and Japanese Civilizations*. New York: Harcourt, Brace, Jovanovich, Inc., 1990.

Spate, Oscar. *The Pacific Since Magellan*. 2 vols. Minneapolis: University of Minnesota Press, 1983.

Van Over, Raymond, ed. *A Treasury of Chinese Literature*. New York: Fawcett Books, 1990.

UNIT TWO

The Seaborne Barbarians: Incursions by the West

OVERVIEW

The Europeans who began regular voyaging across the Indian Ocean into Pacific Asia were bent mainly on establishing independent sources and highly lucrative trade networks for Southeast Asian spices and other commodities. Chinese goods were also in strong demand in Europe, but the West had little to offer that was of interest to the Chinese. With their superior technology in arms and industry, the Europeans were able to quell and subvert local populations in many parts of Pacific Asia.

By the nineteenth century, British commercial power far exceeded that of other nations and became the vanguard of the West's clash with China, particularly in the sale of opium to the Chinese. Through a series of initial miscalculations on both sides, the two countries fought a small scale, coastal war, the first Opium War, that revealed the extreme vulnerability of the Chinese to the superior firepower of British ships. The "unequal treaties" that followed have reverberated through Chinese politics and society ever since. Even in the 1990s, the Chinese government has found it useful to commemorate and publicize the injustices the country bore as a result of the Opium Wars.

China's nineteenth century reform efforts failed due to lack of suitable leadership, a lack of money due to repeated foreign indemnities that were heaped upon it, and the interest paid on foreign loans. New taxes could not be imposed on an already impoverished population.

In Southeast Asia, rivalries among the European powers gained momentum, resulting in the toppling or manipulation of most kingdoms with the exception of Thailand. The trade in opium was not limited to the British in China. Although it is not specifically noted in the text, the Dutch in Southeast Asia, notably in Indonesia, promoted a significant opium trade with the population, aided by Chinese intermediaries. Meanwhile, technological change and new levels of exposure to the West began to alter the social life of Asian cities and to offer new visions of the future to the next generation of Asia leaders.

STUDY RESOURCES

Video: "The Two Coasts of China: Asia and the Challenge of the West"

Text: Chapter 2: *The Seaborne Barbarians: Incursions by the West*

STUDY FOCUS

After viewing the video and reading Chapter 2, you should have a basic understanding of how:

1. European rivalries affected Western imperialism in Asia.

2. An extensive Indo-Pacific system of maritime trade routes vied with those of the early European arrivals.

3. Contact in the modern era between Europe and Asia was a collision of cultures.

4. Foreign powers sought to impose "advanced" Western civilization upon the "inferior" peoples and cultures of Asia.

5. Although a late arrival, the United States also became an imperial power in Pacific Asia.

6. Pressures from the West altered and sometimes overthrew kingdoms in Asia.

KEY CONCEPTS AND NAMES

This is a list of important terms, people, and places that you should understand from reading the text. If you cannot think of a brief explanation for everything on this list, you need to read the text again.

Batavia (Jakarta)
British East India Company
Canton Trade
Chulalongkorn (Rama V)
Cixi
Cochinchina
Coolie Trade
Guangzhou (Canton)
Hong Kong
Imperialism
Industrial Revolution
Li Hongzhang

Macao
Manila Galleon
King Mongkut
Nanjing, Treaty of
Opium Wars
Qing Dynasty
Siam (Thailand)
Spice Trade
Stamford Raffles
Unequal Treaties
VOC

GLOSSARY

■ General

British East India Company: Founded in 1600 and dissolved in 1858 by the queen of England. Also known as The (Honourable) Company. The initial purpose of the Company was to expand English trade as far as the Indian Ocean. Later, the Company expanded British trade into Southeast Asia; it also extended trade into China.

Dutch East India Company: Founded in 1602; also known as the VOC. The Dutch East India Company strove to establish a monopoly in the Spice Trade. It also attempted to control trade in Indonesia by expelling the Portuguese and resisting British encroachment. When the VOC's charter lapsed in 1799, the Dutch state took control of the remnants.

Extraterritoriality: The idea that the laws of a foreign country would be applied to its nationals in other sovereign states. For example, if a British citizen committed a crime on Chinese soil, he would be under the jurisdiction of British law, not Chinese law. Any trial or punishment would be administered by the British, not the Chinese. Extraterritoriality did not end until the twentieth century.

VOC: Acronym of "Vereenigde Oost-Indische Compagnie," which is Dutch for "Dutch East India Company."

Westernization: Term used to describe the process of a country coming under Western influence and adapting features learned from the West. Westernization should not be confused with modernization.

■ China

Canton Trade: Before the Opium Wars, Canton (Guangzhou) was the only point of entry for British trade with China. It was the center for all foreign trade with China until more treaty ports were opened.

Cohong: "Combined merchant companies." A guild of officially authorized Chinese merchants, licensed by the Qing government. The Cohong monopolized foreign trade, and became the major stumbling block for foreign traders in the Canton trade. The Cohong were abolished in 1842 under the Treaty of Nanking.

Factory: (Godown) The "factories" of the China trade were not industrial plants; they were a combination of warehouses, shipping and receiving centers, trading centers, and residences. Godown is from Malay *gudang*, meaning "warehouse."

Foreign Concessions: Refers to the parcels of land ceded to foreign powers in Chinese cities. Within these compounds, each foreign power enforced its own laws with its own police force. The best-known concessions were in Shanghai. The concessions were both a source of employment for Chinese and a haven from Qing authority. Foreign concessions reverted to Chinese control in 1949.

Guangzhou: (gwong joe) Also known as Canton, Guangzhou is a major port city in southern China. It is the capital of Guangdong Province.

Hakka: (hock gah) Literally, "Guest Families." The Hakka are a seafaring Han people who live in southern China, noticeable for their distinctive black apparel and broad-brimmed hats. They were not considered Han Chinese until recently, hence the term "Guest Families." The name "Hong Kong" comes from the Hakka language, which is markedly different from both Cantonese and Mandarin.

Hong Kong: The British Crown colony on the eastern side of the mouth of the Pearl River. Hong Kong is the name for both the principal island of the colony and the colony itself. Hong Kong is Hakka for "Fragrant Harbor;" this is "Xianggang" in Mandarin. The 99-year lease of the New Territories expires on June 1, 1997, at which point the British will return all of Hong Kong to the People's Republic of China.

Li Hongzhang: (lee hung jahng) 1823-1901. A Chinese Viceroy who served the Qing government in many high positions in the second half of the nineteenth century, Li was the diplomatic voice of the Qing.

Lin Zexu: (lynn tsuh shoe) 1785-1850. A Chinese scholar-official who served the Qing government. In 1838, he was sent to Guangzhou to end the opium trade. His successful efforts resulted in the Opium War.

Macao: Established in 1557 by the Portuguese, Macao was the first permanent Western outpost in Asia. It is at the west end of the mouth of the Pearl River. "Macao" is a corruption of "A-Ma-Kao," meaning "The Bay of A-Ma." A-Ma is a guardian of fishermen in Chinese mythology.

Nanjing, Treaty of: The treaty which ended the First Opium War. Negotiated between the British and the Qing in 1842, it was the first Western-style treaty signed by China.

Opium Wars: Wars between Western powers and China that were fought on the pretext of Chinese opposition to the opium trade, but also involved broader issues such as extraterritoriality, tariffs, trading rights, opening of ports, diplomatic relations, and the cultural collision between the West and China.

Shanghai: A port city on the East China Sea, Shanghai was opened as a treaty port to foreign concessions as a result of the First Opium War.

Whanghia, Treaty of: Signed in 1844 between China and the US, it extended the terms of Treaty of Nanjing to the United States. The treaty was negotiated in Whanghia, a small village near Macao.

Zeng Guofan: (tsung gwoe fahn) 1811-1872. A strict Confucian Viceroy who served the Qing government in a variety of posts, Zeng advocated adoption of Western technology and military organization.

■ Southeast Asia

Batavia: Now known as Jakarta, Batavia was site of the Dutch headquarters on Java.

Chulalongkorn: 1853-1910. King of Siam from 1868 to 1910; ruled as Rama V. Chulalongkorn received both traditional and Western schooling. He was unable to exert his power as king in his younger years; however, when older, he instigated reforms that radically modernized Siam. Under Chulalongkorn, Siam was forced to cede territory to Western powers but retained its independence.

Cochinchina: The first French colony in Southeast Asia. Cochinchina was the name for a southern Vietnamese province on the Mekong delta.

Mongkut: 1804-1868. King of Siam from 1851 to 1868; ruled as Rama IV. A devout Buddhist and enthusiastic scholar, Mongkut studied many languages of Asia, as well as Latin and English. He was fascinated by Western science, and read as much as he could about foreign countries.

Mongkut dedicated himself to improving international relations. He also strove to modernize Siam; he implemented legal reforms, promoted modern medicine, and established a royal mint. A strong king, his leadership and ability preserved the integrity of the Thai state.

Saigon: An ancient port city in the Mekong delta of Vietnam. After 1859, Saigon became the French center of Cochinchina.

Saigon, Treaty of: The treaty signed in June 1862 among Vietnam, Spain, and France. The treaty ceded territory to France (establishing Cochinchina) and arranged payment of an indemnity to Spain. This marked the beginning of French encroachment into Southeast Asia.

Spice Islands: Refers to certain islands of modern Indonesia, famed for their bounty of spices. The Dutch exploited these islands' resources.

Straits Settlements: The ports of Malacca, Pinang, and Singapore were collectively known as the Straits Settlements. These were key ports controlled by the British, all located along the Strait of Malacca.

TIME-FRAME QUESTIONS

1. a. Lord Amherst arrives in Beijing
    b. Opium War begins
    c. Lord Macartney arrives in Beijing
    d. British burn the Summer Palace
    e. Lord Napier arrives in Beijing

2. a. British lose American Revolutionary War
    b. British defeat Spanish Armada
    c. Pope divides world between Portugal and Spain
    d. Constantinople falls to Turks
    e. Spanish take Manila

3. a. Dutch dominate trade in Southeast Asia
    b. Opium smoking introduced to China
    c. Cook's voyages of discovery in the Pacific
    d. British East India Company formed
    e. Columbus sails to the New World

40

4. a. British capture Java
   b. King Mongkut signs treaty with British
   c. British take Burma
   d. Chinese cede Hong Kong to Britain
   e. British opens the Suez Canal

5. a. Gold discovered at Sutter's Mill
   b. American Civil War begins
   c. US purchases Alaska from Russia
   d. US annexes Hawaii
   e. Caleb Cushing concludes Treaty of Whanghia

6. a. Robert Hart and Pin Zhun arrive in Europe
   b. American whaling ships arrive in Pacific
   c. Perry arrives in Japan
   d. Magellan arrives in the Philippines
   e. Matteo Ricci arrives in Macao

7. a. Norodom concludes agreement with France
   b. Opening of Japan
   c. French conclude Treaty of Saigon
   d. Dissolution of the British East India Company
   e. Death of King Mongkut

8. a. Opening of Korea
   b. Germany appropriates Shandong
   c. Chulalongkorn ascends to the Siamese throne
   d. Sir Stamford Raffles founds Singapore
   e. Treaty of the Bogue

9. a. Clive's victory at Plassey
   b. Portuguese establish colony of Macao
   c. Reuter founds telegraph agency
   d. Shogunate prohibits export of silver
   e. Chulalongkorn's second visit to Europe

QUESTIONS FOR REVIEW

1. Look at the list of Key Concepts and Names for this chapter. Find all place names, then locate each place on the maps in the text. Pay particular attention to: Spice Islands, silver trade, and the location and dates of imperial conquest by Western powers.

2. How important was opium to the Opium Wars?

3. Discuss the factors that affected Sino-British relations, both before and after the Opium Wars.

4. How did the Siamese response to the West differ from the Chinese response? What were factors in the Siamese ability to respond differently from its neighbors?

5. How did the Malay view of piracy differ from the Western view?

6. The Treaty of Nanjing has been called revolutionary. What made it "revolutionary?" What were the effects of this treaty on China? What kind of precedent did it set for China? for Asia?

7. What tensions developed in the Philippines as a result of the Spanish presence? Why?

8. Why was Chinese immigration to America a source of friction in the American West? What problems do present-day Asian-Americans face? Is there a connection between past attitudes and present ones?

9. Although the Dutch had a long history in Indonesia and Southeast Asia, they eventually ceased to be important in the area. Why?

10. What led to the establishment of the British Crown Colony of Hong Kong? What made Hong Kong attractive to the British? What advantages does Hong Kong possess?

11. Although the British were not the first Europeans in Southeast Asia, they certainly became the most dominant. Why? How?

12. What areas in Southeast Asia were subject to French incursions? Why were the French there? What did they accomplish?

13. Compare and contrast the 1821 Terranova case and the 1839 murder of a Chinese man by British soldiers. What were the responses of the Americans and the British? Why did they respond differently? What major event did the 1839 case ultimately precipitate? Why?

ADDITIONAL RECOMMENDED READINGS

Cipolla, Carlo M. *Guns, Sails, and Empires: Technological Innovation and the Early Phases of European Expansion 1400-1700.* New York: Pantheon, 1960.

Fairbank, John K. *The Chinese World Order: Traditional China's Foreign Relations.* Cambridge: Harvard University Press, 1968.

Israel, Jonathan I. *Dutch Primacy in World Trade, 1585-1740*. Oxford: Clarendon Press, 1989.

Lash, Donald F. *Asia in the Making of Europe*. 2 vols. Chicago: University of Chicago Press, 1965-77.

Spate, Oscar. *The Pacific Since Magellan*. 2 vols. Minneapolis: University of Minnesota Press, 1983.

Spence, Jonathan D. *The Death of Woman Wang*. New York: Penguin Books, Viking Press, 1986.

Wyatt, David K. and Woodside, Alexander. *Moral Order and the Question of Change: Essays on Southeast Asian Thought*. New Haven: Yale University, 1982.

43

UNIT THREE

Meiji: Japan in the Age of Imperialism

OVERVIEW

This unit examines the events and issues of the Meiji Restoration. It does so not just in terms of what the Meiji Restoration meant to Japan, but also how it affected other countries in the Pacific region.

The very name for the Meiji Restoration itself is controversial. The textbook chapter refers to Meiji as one of the five great revolutions of modern times, yet there are those who would not call it a revolution at all. In Japanese it is called Meiji *Ishin*. The word *Ishin* really means a *renewal*, rather than a restoration. Another word in Japanese used to suggest the great cultural changes that went on at that time is *yonaoshi*. This literally means a change in the world, a change by reconstructing and correcting the world around you.

The debates about the nature of the changes that took place in nineteenth century Japan will continue, but the larger questions have to do with the long-term impact on Japanese society and Pacific Asia. Japan's neighbors came to be both inspired and threatened by its modernization, but could not immediately emulate its success. Some reasons why this was so are noted in the textbook, but they too continue to be debated.

Specifically, this chapter asks, "Why was Japan able to modernize so much more successfully than China?" As we follow the course of Japan's development, we begin to see that what may have been deemed the disadvantages of Tokugawa society were, in fact, advantages--for behind the gates of the Shogun's closed country (*sakoku*) lay a society capable of rapid change. Below is a list of some of the differences that may have been critical in determining the responses of China and Japan.

Geography: Japan's smaller size made it easier for a strong central government to control regional rivals. China's government had to expend enormous resources in subduing widespread and sometimes far-off rebellions at a time when its authority was weakening. In addition, Japan's Far East location, furthest from Europe by means of traditional maritime routes, had the effect of insulating the country from the West.

Western Interference: The imperialist powers initially by-passed Japan in favor of the profit they knew could be gained in China. From the outset there was far less impulse to interfere in Japan's internal affairs than in China's. Thus, Japan's modernization occurred at an auspicious "moment in time."

Receptivity: For the Chinese, more than two thousand years of assumed cultural superiority was a habit hard to break. Perhaps only the Western colonizers themselves exceeded them in this conceit. Japan, by contrast, had assimilated outside influences from China and Korea periodically. Cultural borrowing was not anathema to the Japanese. They were, in fact, capable of carrying it to great heights.

Leadership: The administrative talent of the samurai class proved critical to the emergence of Japan as an industrial nation. They offered an "alternative leadership" to the Shogun and the *daimyo*. Used to competition and valuing traits that included boldness and daring, they were able to take risks and seize opportunities that laid the foundations of large modern businesses as well as modernized military forces. China's leadership, by contrast, remained a unitary edifice of the monarchy and the scholar-gentry, neither of which wished to upset the equilibrium by defying their traditional (and usually successful) "defensive" response to barbarian invaders. They believed Westerners could be contained in the treaty ports and used, much as they had co-opted foreign intruders throughout much of Chinese history on the far-off frontiers of Central Asia.

There is also a continuing theme from the previous chapter that will surface periodically throughout this book. That is the insistence by the West that Asian societies become "involved" in global affairs, partaking of the open trading system, offering ports and markets or joining world-wide political alliances. Although ultimately Japan was the most adaptive in its response to challenges from the West in the mid-nineteenth century, its initial reaction to the arrival of the foreigners was similar to that of China and Korea: "expel the barbarian."

STUDY RESOURCES

Video: "The Meiji Revolution"
Text: Chapter 3: *Meiji: Japan in the Age of Imperialism*

STUDY FOCUS

After viewing the video and reading Chapter 3, you should have a basic understanding of the following concepts.

1.   At the time of Perry's mission, the Tokugawa Shogunate was already declining. The additional pressure from outside forced Japan to change.

2.   At the end of the Qing dynasty, China's internal turmoil inhibited the development of an effective response to the incursions of the Western powers.

3.   Korea unsuccessfully tried to keep its borders closed to the outside world. After going to war with China, then Russia, Japan forced Korea into an unequal relationship, and eventually annexed it.

4.   The Western powers served as catalysts for inevitable change in Asia; they were not the cause of change.

KEY CONCEPTS AND NAMES

This is a list of important terms, people, and places that you should understand from reading the text. If you cannot think of a brief explanation for everything on this list, you need to read the text again.

Bakufu
Bakumatsu
Boxers
Cixi
Fukuzawa Yukichi
Han
Ito Hirobumi
Kanagawa, Treaty of
Kanghwa, Treaty of
Kapsin Coup
King Kojong
Li Hongzhang
Meiji

Queen Min
Matthew Perry
Qing Dynasty
Russo-Japanese War
Ryukyu Islands
Sat-Cho
Shimonoseki, Treaty of
Sino-Japanese War
Taewon'gun
Taiping Rebellion
Tonghak
Townsend Harris
Yamagata Aritomo

GLOSSARY

■ General

Kanagawa, Treaty of: Signed on 31 March 1854, after Commodore Perry returned to Japan, the Treaty of Kanagawa was Japan's first treaty with a Western nation. This treaty opened Hakodate and Shimoda to US vessels, and guaranteed that shipwrecked sailors would be treated well.

Kanghwa, Treaty of: Signed on 26 February 1876 between Japan and Korea, this treaty was Korea's first modern, Western-style treaty. Its provisions included opening ports for trade and recognition of Korea as an independent country. It both ended Chinese "monopolization" of Korea and marked the end of Korea's isolation as "the Hermit Kingdom."

Portsmouth, Treaty of: Signed on 5 September 1905 and negotiated by Theodore Roosevelt, this treaty ended the Russo-Japanese War. Japan benefitted greatly from this treaty, at the expense of China, Korea, and Russia.

Russo-Japanese War: 1904-05. Japan was the unexpected victor of this war. Victory raised the prestige of Japan in the world and established it as an imperialist power. This war confirmed Japanese authority in Korea; Japan also gained Russian holdings in China and Manchuria, as well as southern Sakhalin and the Kurile chain. The Treaty of Portsmouth ended the Russo-Japanese War.

Shimonoseki, Treaty of: Signed on 17 April 1895, this treaty ended the first Sino-Japanese War. Negotiated between Ito Hirobumi for Japan and Li Hongzhang for China, it gave Japan extensive concessions, as well as a massive indemnity. Although Japan was forced by the Western powers to give up some of its gains, this treaty established Japan as the foremost power in East Asia.

Sino-Japanese War: 1894-95. After increasing tensions of which country had the "right" to dominate Korea, China and Japan fought a brief war over the issue. Although Western powers expected China to win, Japan easily defeated the Chinese. Even when China sued for peace, Japan kept fighting. Finally, the Treaty of Shimonoseki was negotiated to end the war. China paid a high price for peace, ceding territory and paying a huge indemnity.

Yellow Peril: A popular term that referred to the perceived "menace" that the Chinese and Japanese presented to the West, both in Asia and at home.

■ China

Boxers: Known in Mandarin Chinese as *Yihetuan*, "Righteous and Harmonious Society," which was derived from *Yihequan*, "Righteous and Harmonious Fists" (hence the name "Boxers"). The Boxers were a combination of anti-foreign, anti-Qing, and anti-Christian components, with the anti-foreign element strongest.

In 1900, Boxers attacked foreign legations in Beijing and Tianjin. Foreign troops fought back, took both cities, and sacked Beijing. Li Hongzhang negotiated a settlement with the West, which severely punished China.

Cixi: (tsuh she) 1835-1908. Imperial concubine and Empress Dowager during late Qing China.

In 1861, Cixi's son was made emperor and she, his regent. Although another concubine was appointed co-regent, Cixi deposed her in 1865. Cixi became sole regent and exercised supreme power.

In 1875, Cixi's son (the Emperor) died. Violating the established procedures for succession, she installed her three-year-old nephew as emperor. During her nephew's reign, Cixi continued to rule with absolute authority. She did not relinquish power until her death.

Taiping Rebellion: 1850-1864. Literally, "Great Harmony," usually translated as "Great Peace."

Led by Hong Xiuquan, who combined anti-Confucianism with quasi-Christian theories, the Taiping Rebellion was a powerful assault on the Qing dynasty. The Taipings developed out of various frustrations, ranging from dissatisfied minority peoples to reactions against the increasing presence of foreigners in China. The Taiping Rebellion seriously weakened China at a time when it faced increasing pressures, both internal and external.

■ Japan

Bakufu: (bah coo foo) The government of the Shogun.

Bakumatsu: (bah coo ma tsoo) The final years of the Tokugawa Shogunate. 1853-1868.

"Black Ships": Refers to the ships of Commodore Perry; by extension, represents unwelcome foreign pressure.

Daimyo: (die myo) Daimyo were the rulers of the *han* of Tokugawa Japan.

Diet: The Japanese parliament, created in 1890.

Edo: (eh doe) Originally a small fishing village, Edo was the Tokugawa capital from 1603 to 1867. In 1868, the emperor was relocated to Edo; it became the new capital and was renamed Tokyo ("Eastern Capital.")

Fukoku Kyohei: (foo co coo kyo hay) "Enrich the Nation, Strengthen the Army." A Meiji period slogan used to spur the modernization of Japan.

Genro: Literally, "Original Elders." Refers to the older Meiji statesmen, namely: Ito Hirobumi, Kuroda Kiyotaka, Matsukata Masayoshi, Oyama Iwao, Saigo Tsugumichi, Yamagata Aritomo, and Inoue Kaoru.

Hakodate: (hah co dah tay) One of two ports initially opened with the Treaty of Kanagawa, Hakodate is located in southern Hokkaido.

Han: (hahn) "Domain." The regions controlled by daimyo.

Meiji: (may gee) Literally, "Enlightened Rule." The reign name of Mutsuhito. Also the name of the period during which Mutsuhito was emperor, which was 1868 to 1912.

Mikado: (me caw doe) A Japanese term for the Japanese emperor.

Mutsuhito: (moo tsoo he toe) Emperor Meiji's given name.

Ryukyu Islands: A chain of islands that stretches between Kyushu and Taiwan, the Ryukyus are part of Okinawa Prefecture. Also known as the Liuchiu Islands.

Sat-Cho: A combination of the *han* names "Satsuma" and "Choshu," these *han* allied with each other against the Tokugawa.

Shimoda: One of two ports initially opened under the terms of the Kanagawa Treaty, Shimoda is on the tip of the Izu peninsula, southwest of Tokyo.

Shishi: (she she) "Men of Spirit." A term for the samurai who opposed--often violently--the changes wrought upon Japan by both the *bakumatsu* Tokugawa and by the Meiji government. They also opposed opening the country to the West. Self-righteous and dogmatic, they were the predecessors to later ultranationalists.

Shizoku: (she zoe coo) A term for the samurai class.

Sonno Joi: (sewn no joe ee) "Revere the Emperor; Expel the Barbarians." This phrase was the foundation of the philosophy of the *shishi*.

Tokugawa: The family name of the last Shoguns. The Tokugawa, who ruled Japan from 1600 to 1867, imposed both a lasting peace and a policy of isolation on Japan.

Tozama: (toe zah ma) "Outside Lord." Refers to the daimyo and *han* that were not aligned with the Tokugawa before the Battle of Shimonoseki.

Yokohama: Port city southwest of Tokyo; capital of Kanagawa Prefecture. As part of the Treaty of Kanagawa, Yokohama was opened to foreign trade in 1858.

Zaibatsu: Business and industrial conglomerates that developed through cooperation with the government.

■ Korea

Kapsin Coup: Occurred on 4 December 1884; led primarily by Kim Ok-kyun. Korean reformers, with Japanese backing, killed several members of the Korean royal family and took control of the palace. On 5 December, a new government was declared. However, Chinese troops ousted the rebels from the palace; the rebels retreated under Japanese protection. The Chinese restored the old government, and the coup ended in failure. Still, the coup led to further tensions between China and Japan over the issue of Korea; these tensions were temporarily resolved by the 1885 Convention of Tianjin.

King Kojong: 1852-1919; reigned 1864-1907. Kojong is the posthumous name of Yi Myong-bok, the twenty-sixth king of the Yi house of Korea. A regency ruled for Kojong until his marriage to Queen Min in 1866, but Kojong's power was limited until the fall of the *Taewon'gun* in 1873.

Kojong sought to bring Korea to the modern world, and the pinnacle of his foreign policy was the signing of the Treaty of Kanghwa. However, Kojong was a conservative traditionalist, and he abandoned many of the reforms instituted by his father, the *Taewon'gun*.

Kojong was reduced to a figurehead in 1884. Forced to abdicate by the Japanese in 1907, Kojong was succeeded by his son, Sunjong, and lived out his life in retirement.

Sohak: Literally, "Western Learning." Used from the late eighteenth century to refer to Roman Catholicism; *Sohak* can also refer to Western science. Although *Sohak* and Western books were banned, there were more than 20,000 Korean Catholics by 1860.

Taewon'gun: (teh wahn goon) "Grand Prince." Although *Taewon'gun* is a royal title for the father of a king, the term is commonly used for a specific person, namely Yi Ha-ung (1820-1898), father of King Kojong. The *Taewon'gun* ruled Korea from 1864 to 1873.

Tonghak: "Eastern Learning." *Tonghak* was a religious movement, founded in 1860 by Ch'oe Che-u, that grew into a political movement.

Yangban: (yahng bahn) The educated ruling class of Yi Korea.

■ United States

Townsend Harris: 1804-1878. First American consul in Japan. According to the Treaty of Kanagawa, there was to be an American consular representative stationed in Japan; Townsend Harris was the first to fill that position.

From his arrival in Japan in 1856, Harris negotiated with the Japanese. He was rewarded with a commercial treaty in 1858. Harris continued in Japan as the US representative. However, when his health declined, Harris asked to be relieved of his duties, and left Japan in 1862.

Matthew Calbraith Perry: 1794-1858. In March 1852, Commodore Perry of the US Navy was assigned command of four ships. His mission: to establish relations with Japan. Perry and his ships reached Japan in July 1853. On 14 July 1853, he presented Japanese officials a letter from President Millard Fillmore, which asked for the establishment of relations and trade. Perry also emphasized the importance of avoiding confrontation between the two countries. Shortly thereafter, he and his ships left. Before leaving, he told the Japanese he would be back with a larger contingent to receive their reply.

Perry returned to Japan in February 1854, this time with eight ships. On 31 March 1854, the Treaty of Kanagawa was signed, which was both Japan's first treaty with a Western power and the death knell of the Tokugawa policy of isolation.

TIME-FRAME QUESTIONS

1. a. Sino-Japanese War
   b. World War I
   c. US Civil War
   d. First Opium War
   e. Russo-Japanese War

2. a. Li-Lobanov Agreement
   b. Treaty of Kanghwa
   c. Treaty of Shimonoseki
   d. Treaty of Tianjin
   e. Treaty of Kanagawa

3. a. Satsuma Rebellion
   b. Japan Establishes Conscript Army
   c. Taiping Rebellion Begins
   d. Kapsin Coup
   e. Japanese Expedition to Taiwan

4. a. Meiji Constitution
   b. Japan Eliminates Extraterritoriality
   c. Meiji Era Begins
   d. Ch'oe Che-u Founds Tonghak
   e. Boxer Rebellion

5. a. Ito Hirobumi Assassinated
   b. Cixi Dies
   c. Queen Min Assassinated
   d. Emperor Meiji Dies
   e. Kim Ok-kyun Assassinated

QUESTIONS FOR REVIEW

1. Look at the list of Key Concepts and Names for this chapter. Find all place names, then locate each place on the maps in the text. Note in particular military interaction between the West and Japan and China.

2. Commodore Perry's impressions of Japan were, in part, of a society that was frozen in time. But how isolated was Japan? To what degree was it already changing and to what degree was Perry's visit responsible for changing it further?

3. Regular Western contact and trade with China came sooner than with Japan. However, the pattern of Western interactions with the two countries was completely different. Why? What factors effected each countries' ability to handle pressures from the West?

4. How did the Russo-Japanese War effect Japan's status in Asia? in Europe? in Japan itself?

5. Where did the initial resistance to Tokugawa rule begin? Why did it begin in those areas?

6. If Japan was an example to the rest of Asia in its resistance to Western colonial expansion, how can we account for Japanese imperialism in Korea and China?

7. Who was Ito Hirobumi? What was his role in Meiji Japan?

8. What was the Kapsin Coup? Was it successful? What was its effect on regional relations?

9. Who was Li Hongzhang? What were his views on "modernization?" How successful was he?

10. What were the political factors in Asia (and Europe) that led Great Britain and Meiji Japan to ally with one another?

11. What events led to the first Sino-Japanese War? What effect did this war have on Sino-Japanese relations? What effect did it have on relations between Japan and Korea? What effect did it have on Western perceptions of Japan? of China?

12. Who was Fukuzawa Yukichi? What were his accomplishments?

13. How did events in China in the mid-nineteenth century influence Japanese thinking about how to handle the West?

14. What was Korea's response to the West? How did it respond to attempted incursions by the West? Why?

ADDITIONAL RECOMMENDED READINGS

Eckert, Carter J. and Ki-baik Lee. *Korea Old and New: A History.* Cambridge: Harvard University Press, 1990. (Chapters 12-14)

Hsu, Immanuel C.Y. *The Rise of Modern China.* New York: Oxford University Press, 1990.

Jansen, Marius B. and Gilbert Rozman. *Japan in Transition, from Tokugawa to Meiji.* Princeton: Princeton University Press, 1986.

Natsume, Soseki. *Kokoro.* Trans. Edwin McClellan. Chicago: Gateway Editions, 1985. (Fiction by Japan's most popular author.)

Wray, Harry and Hilary F. Conroy. *Japan Examined: Perspectives on Modern Japanese History.* Honolulu: University of Hawaii Press, 1983.

UNIT FOUR

The Rise of Nationalism and Communism

OVERVIEW

Japan's Meiji transformation produced a series of aftershocks throughout East Asia as traditional societies strove to adjust to the impact of new ideas and technologies among them. All the while a stream of new influences, religious and ideological missionaries, political representatives, and new economic colonizers poured across to Pacific ports from Europe and increasingly from the United States. The imperative to modernize was most keenly felt by a new generation of intellectuals whose thinking was shaped both by their traditional upbringing and their access to Western education and ideas.

The changes they contemplated were as much cultural as political or economic. They involved massive transformations even in basic language and expression, as in China, Korea, and Vietnam, where the gulf between the historic language of the intelligentsia and popular expression at the beginning of the nineteenth century was in many ways as wide as the gap between the Latin-speaking clerks of the early European Renaissance and the mass of barely literate vernacular-speakers below them. Everywhere the same questions were pondered: What can be taken from the West? How can it be used? How can it be resisted?

At the same time, the affluence produced by Western technology made more extreme the contrast with the desperate poverty of the mass of Asia/Pacific peoples--those who flocked to the new urban factories were often worse off than the peasant relatives they had left at home. Thoughtful students and young reformers came to ponder these inequities--and many blamed the West for the huge gap between expectation and reality.

Far-off events cast their shadows. Nowhere was the post-World War I collapse of Wilsonian idealism felt more keenly than in Asia's Pacific cities. In 1919 crowds of nationalist demonstrators took to the streets in Korea and China to protest the results of the Versailles Treaty. These frustrations were but a part of the complex interaction of forces that were building in domestic and international politics. The prelude to war began in China where Japan's military leaders succeeded in thrusting their country on a path toward dominance in Asia and confrontation with the Western anti-Fascist democracies.

STUDY RESOURCES

Video: "From the Barrel of a Gun"
Text: Chapter 4: *The Rise of Nationalism and Communism*

STUDY FOCUS

After viewing the video and reading Chapter 4, you should have a basic understanding of the following concepts.

1.   Nationalism grew and developed throughout Pacific Asia in the late nineteenth and early twentieth centuries.

2.   Communism was a powerful force in all the countries of Pacific Asia, albeit in different ways. Idealism, nationalism, and anti-imperialism all influenced communist movements.

3.   The reaction in Asia to the Treaty of Versailles demonstrated how Asian visions of Asia's future clashed with the Western, Eurocentric vision of the world.

4.   The failure to implement Wilsonian ideals, in conjunction with the Versailles Treaty in 1919, contributed to militant nationalism in Asia.

5.   Anti-colonial and independence movements grew in number and intensity during the early twentieth century.

6.   Along with new ideologies, armed forces and militarism were instrumental in shaping modern Pacific Asia.

7.   Japanese colonialism expanded in Asia in the decades before WWII.

8.   Nationalist movements often required charismatic leaders such as Ho Chi Minh and Sukarno to serve as rallying points.

KEY CONCEPTS AND NAMES

This is a list of important terms, people, and places that you should understand from reading the text. If you cannot think of a brief explanation for everything on this list, you need to read the text again.

Emilio Aguinaldo	March First Movement
Chiang Kai-shek	Marco Polo Bridge Incident
Chinese Communist Party (CCP)	May Fourth Movement
Communism	Mukden Incident
Dong Du Movement	Nationalism
Guomindang (KMT)	1919
Mohammad Hatta	Syngman Rhee
Ho Chi Minh	Sukarno
Independence Club	Sun Yat-sen
Katipunan	Versailles Treaty
Kwantung Army	Warlords
Manchuria	Washington Conference

GLOSSARY

■ General

Comintern: Abbreviation for the Third Communist International. This group was founded in in the USSR in 1919. It was formed to coordinate communist parties worldwide.

French Indochina: Refers to the area of French colonialism in Southeast Asia: Cambodia, Laos, Vietnam, and part of southern China. "Indochina" refers to Indian and Chinese influences in the area. However, because the term "Indochina" ignores native culture, and is also a reminder of French imperialism, it has fallen into disuse. Usually, the more neutral "Southeast Asia" is employed. Although "French Indochina" is useful as a historical term, that area is commonly called "mainland (or peninsular) Southeast Asia."

Manchukuo: The name of the puppet state set up and controlled by the Japanese in Manchuria. The Mukden Incident set the stage for the establishment of Manchukuo. The head of state was Puyi, the deposed emperor of China. Manchukuo existed from 1932 to 1945.

Manchuria: An area of northeastern China. Rich in natural resources, Manchuria was an area of contention among imperial powers. It is also the homeland of the Manchus, who established the Qing dynasty.

Marco Polo Bridge Incident: On the night of 7 July 1937, shots were fired at a railroad bridge southwest of Beijing. Whether the initial fire came from Japanese or Chinese forces remains unclear to this day, but there is no doubt that this precipitated all-out war in China.

Mukden Incident: Also known as the Manchurian Incident. Refers to the bombing of train tracks on 18 September 1931, by officers of the Kwantung Army. Blaming the Chinese and citing self-defence, the Japanese Army advanced, ultimately occupying Manchuria and establishing the puppet state of Manchukuo.

Nanjing Massacre: Also known as the Rape of Nanjing. In December 1937, Japanese troops invaded Nanjing and brutalized the population. Although this incident has been downplayed in Japan, it remains fresh in Chinese minds and affects Sino-Japanese relations.

Nationalism: The sense of unity and feeling of identity felt by a group of people and characterized by shared culture, language, territory, and traditions.

■ China

Baihua: (buy hwa) Literally, "plain language." A literary movement of the 1920s in China, the main idea of *baihua* was to promote writing as people spoke, rather than using the ancient forms of classical Chinese. Hu Shi, Chen Duxiu, and Lu Xun were all advocates of *baihua*.

Chen Duxiu: (chuhn doo show) 1879-1942. Chen received a classical education; he also studied in Japan. After returning to China, he became a professor at Beijing University. He published a journal, *New Youth*, which promoted radical modernization, *Baihua*, and Marxism. In July 1921, Chen was elected the first Secretary-General of the CCP. He was dismissed in 1927, during a KMT assault against the CCP. Chen never played a role in Chinese politics again. Although he co-founded the CCP, Chen died in obscurity and has been ignored in the PRC.

Chiang Kai-shek: (jahng guy shek) 1887-1975. One of the major political leaders of twentieth century China, Chiang's career included military service and leadership in the Guomindang (1928-49). After the Guomindang's loss to the Communists, he established a government in exile in Taiwan, serving as President of Republic of China (ROC) from 1949-75. Chiang's son, Chiang Ching-kuo, succeeded him as head of the ROC.

Chinese Communist Party (CCP): Secretly founded in Shanghai in July 1921 by Chen Duxiu and representatives of communist groups from all of China, including Mao Zedong. Comintern played a significant role in the foundation of the party.

Guomindang (KMT): (gwoe min dahng) Literally, "National People's Party." The Wade-Giles romanization is Kuomintang, from which KMT is derived; also known as the Nationalists. Founded in 1912 by Sun Yat-sen, the KMT was involved in China's attempts at parliamentary government. Although the KMT and the CCP cooperated initially, they split after Sun died. After losing the Chinese Civil War in 1949, the KMT retreated to Taiwan. The KMT claims to be the legitimate government of all China.

Hu Shi: (who sure) 1891-1962. Educated in America, Hu became a professor at Beijing University upon his return to China. Hu advocated Western liberalism, *Baihua*, and democratic ideals. Although a critic of China's traditions, Hu favored gradual change, and called for individual solutions to individual problems. Hu was the international voice for the moderate Chinese position.

Li Dazhao: (lee dah jao) 1888-1927. The CCP claims Li as one of its founders, even though he was not at the 1921 organizational meeting. Li, head librarian at Beijing University, was Mao Zedong's mentor and introduced him to Marxism-Leninism.

May Fourth Movement: So named for an incident in Beijing on 4 May 1919, in which about 3000 university students poured into the streets to protest the terms of the Treaty of Versailles. The movement itself is usually given the dates 1917-1921. It was a total rejection of traditional Chinese culture by young, modern-educated Chinese.

May Thirtieth Incident: In the spring of 1925, Chinese workers called a strike against Japanese-owned factories in Shanghai. On 30 May 1925, police of the foreign concessions fired on and killed several student protesters. This led to nationwide boycotts, strikes, and riots.

Nanjing: Literally, "southern capital." The first capital of Ming China. Eventually, the Ming adopted a dual capital system, split between Beijing (administration) and Nanjing (ceremonies). Nanjing was the KMT base, and served as the KMT capital from 1928 to 1937.

New Culture Movement: Often given the dates 1915-1925. The appearance of *New Youth*, published by Chen Duxiu, marks the beginning of this movement. This movement rejected traditional Chinese culture and sought to replace it with something modern.

Northern Expedition: A military maneuver of 1926. The KMT pushed north, to gain control of areas ruled by warlords. The expedition's success established Chiang Kai-shek as virtual dictator of China.

Three Principles of the People: The platform of the KMT at its establishment in 1912. The Three Principles, proposed by Sun Yat-sen, are democracy, people's livelihood, and nationalism.

Warlords: Independent generals of the late Qing and Republic periods. Warlords were regional powers, surviving through their control of territories and command of personal armies.

Xi'an Incident: Refers to the December 1936 capture of Chiang Kai-shek by Zhang Xueliang, a general (supposedly) under his command. Zhang took Chiang in a successful attempt to force the KMT to stop fighting the CCP and create a unified front to fight the Japanese.

Xinhai Revolution: (shin high) Mandarin name for the revolution of 1911. This revolt toppled the Qing but did not replace the dynasty with another central power. China was wracked by civil war until 1949.

Yuan Shikai: (you-ahn sure kai) 1859-1916. Qing general who quelled the 1894 Kapsin Coup and the 1900 Boxer Uprising. The success of the Xinhai Revolution rested upon Yuan's refusal to support the Qing. Yuan became president of the Chinese Republic in 1912. He attempted to establish himself as emperor in 1915. However, this bid for supremacy was rejected by other political forces.

■ Indonesia

Dutch East Indies: Name of the Dutch colony which, along with other territories, became modern Indonesia. The capital was Batavia.

DNS: Acronym for Dutch Native Schools.

Mohamad Hatta: (huh tuh) 1902-1980. Educated in the DNS and in Holland, where he was active in anticolonial politics. Arrested in 1927, he was acquitted; Hatta returned to Batavia in 1932.

Hatta felt that the education of nationalist leaders was more important than the formation of mass parties (which would be easy targets for Dutch suppression). Arrested again in 1935, he was exiled from Java until just before the Japanese invasion. During the war, he served as vice-chair of mass organizations.

In August 1945, he and Sukarno founded Indonesia by declaring independence. Sukarno became president and Hatta, vice-president. Troubled by political trends, Hatta resigned as vice-president in 1956.

Netherlands Indies: Another term for the Dutch East Indies.

PKI: Acronym for *Partai Komunis Indonesia*, the Indonesian communist party. Founded in 1920. The PKI enjoyed mass popularity on Java and Sumatra, but was suppressed by the Dutch. Re-emerging after WWII, the PKI was active until 1966, when it was banned. See Chapters 8, 11.

PNI: Stands for *Partai Nasional Indonesia*, the Indonesian Nationalist Party. Founded by Sukarno in 1927 as an independence-seeking mass party. Dissolved in 1930, it was re-formed in 1945 and was the most important party until 1971, when Sukarno was deposed. PNI became part of the Indonesian Democratic Party in 1973. See Chapters 8, 11.

Priyayi: (pre yuh yee) The traditional educated ruling class of Java.

Sukarno: 1901-1970. Co-founder of the Republic of Indonesia, he was its first president. His greatest legacy was the concept of "Indonesia," a modern nation-state formed from the great diversity of the islands. A popular, nationalist leader, he led a leftist government that allied itself with China and was hostile to Malaysia and the West. Sukarno developed "Guided Democracy." See Chapters 8, 11.

■ Japan

February 26 Incident: Also known as the 2-2-6 Incident. On 26 February 1936, several young army officers, leading about 1800 men, took control of central Tokyo and assassinated several politicians and military officials. Claiming to be acting in the name of the emperor, they called for a "Showa Restoration" and a new government. However, they were denounced as traitors. The rebels surrendered on 29 February; after a secret trial, the officers and their civilian supporters were executed.

Inukai Tsuyoshi: (ee new kai tsoo yo she) 1855-1932. First elected to the Diet in 1890, he served in Japan's parliament until his assassination. Inukai opposed the Sat-Cho clique throughout his career.

When he became prime minister in December 1931, two enormous problems faced him: the Great Depression and the invasion of Manchuria. The military opposed his plans for civilian control of the army; he was assassinated by junior officers on 15 May 1932. This marked the end of civilian government until after WWII.

Taisho Emperor: (tie show) 1879-1926; reigned 1912-1926. His given name was Yoshihito; his reign name was Taisho ("Great Justice"). The first Japanese crown prince to receive a western-style education, he was also the first to travel outside of Japan. During the Taisho era, Japan grew rapidly, on both the domestic and international stages. Sadly, this era was marred by the annexation of Korea in 1910, the Rice Riots of 1918, the Great Kanto Earthquake of 1923, and increasing Japanese interference in China and repression at home.

Yoshihito is said to have suffered from lead poisoning, because of his wet-nurse 's makeup. He was unhealthy his entire life. In 1921, due to the deterioration of the Taisho Emperor's mind, Crown Prince Hirohito was appointed regent. Upon the emperor's death on 25 December 1926, Hirohito ascended to the Chrysanthemum Throne.

■ Korea

Independence Club: A society of *yangban* formed in 1896 by Dr. Philip Jaisohn. Its cause was an independent Korea. It was dissolved in 1898.

Dr. Philip Jaisohn: (Korean name, So Chae-p'il) 1863-1951. So Chae-p'il was born in a *yangban* clan. After studying in Japan he took part in the 1884 Kapsin Coup, after which he fled to the US. In America, he became an MD, converted to Christianity, married an American, and changed his name to Philip Jaisohn. After the 1895 Sino-Japanese War, he returned to Korea. He promoted modernization and independence through both his newspaper and the Independence Club. When conservatives re-established control in 1898, Jaisohn again left for the US, where he practiced medicine, became an American citizen, and continued to work for Korean independence. After WWII, he returned to Korea to advise American occupation forces. However, after Syngman Rhee became the first president of South Korea in 1947, Jaisohn went back to the US. He never again returned to Korea.

■ Philippines

Emilio Aguinaldo: 1869-1964. Prominent nationalist and a leader of the independence movements against Spain and America. Captured by US forces in 1901, he had no role in politics thereafter. Eventually granted amnesty by the US, he lived out his life as a respected leader of the early nationalist movements.

Creoles: Spaniards born in a Spanish colony (such as the Philippines).

Filipino: A term used for natives of the Philippines, most of whom are of Malayan descent.

Ilustrados: Spanish-educated Filipinos, the elite of Filipino society.

Katipunan: (kah tea poo nahn) The shortened name of a peasant-based nationalist society. Founded in 1892 by Andres Bonifacio (1863-1897), this semi-secret society led the rebellions against Spain and the US.

Mestizos: Refers to Filipinos born of mixed heritage, usually a Spanish father and a Philippine mother.

Partido Nacionalista: Officially established in 1907 as an alternative to the US-sanctioned Partido Federal, the Nacionalista (Nationalist) Party was a coalition of Filipino elite associations. The Nacionalistas were based in Manila and opposed to American dominance of the Philippines. The party called for immediate and unconditional independence for the Philippines.

The Partido Nacionalista remained virtually unopposed in Filipino domestic politics until 1946. After WWII, a former member of the party, Manuel Roxas, formed the Partido Liberal and won the first free presidential election. A loose coalition of Nacionalistas and Liberales then dominated Philippine politics until 1972, when the Nacionalistas became inactive under martial law imposed by its leader, Ferdinand Marcos. Today, the Nacionalista Party, headed by Juan Enrile, is again part of a coalition of political parties under the government of Corazon Aquino.

Peninsulares: Refers to Spaniards in a colony who were born in Spain (as opposed to the colonial-born *Creoles*).

Philippine-American War: 1899-1902. For the US, this was a colonial insurrection; for the Philippines, it was a continuation of the struggle for independence against colonial overlords.

In February 1899, fighting broke out between US and Filipino forces. Although the US suffered setbacks in 1900, the capture of guerrilla leader Aguinaldo in March 1901 paved the way for eventual American victory. Both sides suffered heavy casualties. Civilians included, the Philippine loss ratio was over 50 to 1.

Philippine Revolution: 1896-1898. A revolution against the Spanish, launched by *Katipunan* and led by Andres Bonifacio (1862-1897) and Emilio Aguinaldo. The success of this rebellion, combined with the Spanish-American War, drove the Spanish from the Philippines.

Manuel Quezon: 1878-1944. Dominant native political leader and statesman during the American colonial occupation of the Philippines. An *ilustrado*, Quezon came from a loyalist family and consequently did not take part in the Filipino independence movement against the Spanish. However, he was active against the Americans. After imprisonment by US authorities, Quezon became politicized, joined the

Partido Nacionalista, was elected to the Filipino assembly, where he helped to influence American colonial policies. Elected and reelected to the first presidency of the Philippine Commonwealth in 1935 and 1941, Quezon had to flee the islands when the Japanese invaded in 1942. He died in Washington, DC, from tuberculosis.

Jose Rizal: 1861-1896. A patriotic Filipino novelist whose execution sparked the Philippine Revolution of 1896-1898.

Manuel Roxas: 1894-1948. As a member of the Nacionalista Party, Roxas was elected to The Philippines Assembly in the 1920s, where he became Speaker of the Assembly. He opposed Quezon, although they were members of the same party. When the Japanese invaded, Roxas was captured by them and forced to take part in their puppet-government. However, he used this position to assist the Filipino underground. When independence was granted in 1946, Roxas was elected the first President. After two years of an administration marked by corruption, Roxas died in office.

Spanish-American War: 1898. The US victory established American control of Guam, the Philippines, and Puerto Rico; Cuba gained independence from Spain as a result of this war.

Tagalog: (tah gah log) A major language of the northern Philippines and one of the two official languages (the other is English). Until the middle of the twentieth century, Tagalog was rarely spoken outside of the island of Luzon. Since 1960, Tagalog has been the most widely spoken language of the Philippines.

■ Vietnam

Dong Du Movement: (dong doe) Literally, "Eastern Travel." Between 1905 and 1908, many Vietnamese students travelled to Japan to study. The name stems from the relative locations of Japan and Vietnam.

Ho Chi Minh: (hoe gee min) 1890-1969. Pseudonym for Nguyen Sinh Cung. Ho first learned of Marxism when he lived in London during WWI. He attended the Versailles Peace Conference, and demanded independence for Vietnam. Afterwards, Ho co-founded the French Communist Party.

In 1923, Ho studied Marxism in Moscow and worked at Comintern headquarters. In 1924, he went to Guangzhou, to work with the KMT and foster communist activity in French Indochina. Ho left Guangzhou in 1927, to escape Chiang Kai-shek's repression of communists. Ho returned to south China in 1930 and formed the Vietnamese Communist

Party in Hong Kong. It became the Indochinese Communist Party (ICP) in October 1930. Imprisoned by the British in 1931, he was released in 1933 and went to Moscow. He spent the next few years in the USSR.

In 1938, Ho visited CCP headquarters in Yan'an, then trained guerrillas in central China. In May 1941, Ho presided over the formation of the League for the Independence of Vietnam--the Viet Minh. Ho spent most of his time during WWII organizing the Viet Minh and preparing for the revolution that would come after the war.

The Japanese drove the French from Vietnam on 9 March 1945; Japan's surrender on 15 August left a power void. After the Japanese withdrawal, the Viet Minh launched their attack, took Hanoi with ease, and established the Democratic Republic of Vietnam on 2 September 1945. Hanoi was the capital and Ho Chi Minh was the president. After the Viet Minh's rise to power in 1945, members of the ICP and of the Viet Minh were in most of the key posts. The first National Assembly was elected in early 1946; the Assembly reaffirmed Ho as president. Shortly thereafter, Ho made a coalition with rival parties. In December 1946, negotiations with the French broke down; this led to war. After the French defeat at Dien Bien Phu in 1954, an international conference on Vietnam refused to legitimize Ho's government and divided his country at the seventeenth parallel.

After 1954, Ho retained the presidency of the North but actually spent his time promoting Vietnam's interests in the international arena. Ho died of a heart attack on 3 September 1969. As the liberator of his people and the founder of the country, Ho is honored throughout Vietnam and is the symbol of the nation.

Hue: (hue) Located on the Song Huang (Perfume) River, Hue is in central Vietnam, and is a cultural, historical, and religious center.

Indochinese Communist Party: Founded in 1930 as the result of a factional split within the Vietnam Revolutionary League (VRL). Ho Chi Minh, at the instruction of Comintern, reunited the VRL and the communists under the banner of the Indochinese Communist Party (ICP).

After the Viet Minh's rise to power in 1945, members of the ICP and of the Viet Minh were placed in most of the key posts. However, Ho Chi Minh worked out a coalition with rival parties, and the ICP announced its own dissolution in November of that year, to induce noncommunist participation in the new government. In reality, the ICP merely went underground.

In 1946, after the start of the war with France, the ICP reemerged to guide the resistance through its influence on both the government and the Viet Minh.

64

Nguyen Truong To: (win trong doe) 1827- 1871. A Catholic, To had both a traditional education and French tutoring. Although a loyalist to the Vietnamese court, To was a strong advocate of reform; unfortunately, he was unsuccessful in his attempts to modernize Vietnam.

Phan Boi Chau: (fahng boy jao) 1876-1940. Traditionally-educated anti-colonial revolutionary. Although his many attempts to gain independence for Vietnam failed, today he is revered as a patriot.

Phan Chu Trinh: (fahng jew trin) 1872-1926. A nationalist who sought to modernize Vietnam; Trinh devoted himself to Vietnam's independence. Although few Vietnamese agreed with his rejection of violence, Trinh is widely respected as a patriot.

Viet Minh: Shortened form of *Viet Nam Doc Lap Dong Minh Hoi*, literally, "Vietnam People's Independence League." Founded in 1941 by Ho Chi Minh, the Viet Minh was established as a broad political front for Vietnamese nationalism. However, the communists were the most influential faction.

TIME-FRAME QUESTIONS

1. a. February 26 Incident.
   b. Marco Polo Bridge Incident.
   c. May Thirtieth Incident.
   d. Mukden Incident.
   e. March First Movement.

2. a. Washington Conference.
   b. Philippine Act (ended Philippine-American War).
   c. Versailles Treaty.
   d. Foundation of the University of Hanoi.
   e. First congress of the CCP in Shanghai.

3. a. Foundation of KMT.
   b. Formation of the Nacionalista Party.
   c. Foundation of the Vietnamese Nationalist Party.
   d. Foundation of PKI.
   e. Foundation of the Viet Minh.

4. a. Funeral of King Kojong.
   b. Death of Yuan Shikai.
   c. Foundation of PNI.
   d. William McKinley elected President.
   e. Presentation of the Twenty-One Demands.

5. a. Northern Expedition.
   b. Mohammed Hatta returns to Batavia.
   c. Great Kanto Earthquake.
   d. Founding of Dong Kinh Free School.
   e. Korean provisional government-in-exile established.

QUESTIONS FOR REVIEW

1. Look at the list of Key Concepts and Names for this chapter. Find all place names, then locate each place on the maps in the text.

2. What was the significance of 1919 to modern Asia? What events happened in China? in Europe? in Indonesia? in Korea? What individuals were particularly prominent in this year? Why?

3. Imagine you are a Chinese university student in 1919 or 1920. If you were interviewed by a Western journalist, what would you say? What are your hopes for your country? What changes do you want?

4. What role did the Versailles Conference play in the development of Asian nationalism? Why?

5. What role did Western-style education play in decolonization? What was the purpose of such education from the Westerners' point of view? from the natives' point of view? Compare and contrast the roles of the Filipino *Ilustrados*, the Dutch-educated Indonesians, and the French-educated Vietnamese.

6. What factors affected the leaders of early twentieth century Asian political movements? What traits are shared by these leaders? What traits sat them apart?

7. What was the Japanese colonial policy in Korea? How did the two countries' relationship affect Japan's economy? Korea's?

8. What role did Japan play in modernization movements elsewhere in Asia? Which future Asian leaders travelled to Japan? Why?

9. What was the connection between the KMT and the CCP? between Comintern and the CCP? between Ho Chi Minh and Comintern? between Comintern and the KMT? between Ho Chi Minh and the French Communist Party?

10. Were Vietnamese leaders united in their approach to French colonialism? What routes to cultural reform were proposed?

66

11. What was the impact of the agreements made at the Washington Conference? How powerful were these agreements? How were the decisions of the Conference carried out?

12. Who was Phan Boi Chau? What did he accomplish? How?

13. Communism was an important "ism" in Asia. What were other important "isms"?

14. Sun Yat-sen is considered the father of modern China by both the Nationalists and the Communists. Why?

15. Why were the Philippines "severely strained" by the collapse of Spanish rule in Latin America? What happened to the Manila Galleon? Why?

ADDITIONAL RECOMMENDED READINGS

Akutagawa, Ryunosuke. *Rashomon and Other Stories*. Trans. Takashi Kojima. New York: Liveright Publishing Corporation, 1970.

Kim, Richard E. *Lost Names: Scenes from a Boyhood in Japanese-Occupied Korea*. New York: Universe Books, 1988.

Pa Chin. *Family*. Prospect Heights, IL: Waveland Press, 1972.

Stanley, Peter W. *A Nation in the Making: The Philippines and the United States, 1899-1921*. Cambridge: Harvard University Press, 1974.

Steinberg, David Joel, ed. *In Search of Southeast Asia: A Modern History*. Part 3. Honolulu: University of Hawaii Press, 1987.

Wilbur, C. Martin. *Sun Yat-sen, Frustrated Patriot*. New York: Columbia University Press, 1976.

UNIT FIVE

Maelstrom: The Pacific War and Its Aftermath

OVERVIEW

Japan's belief in its "special position" in Asia collided with the United States' perception that its own security interests in the Pacific were linked to its commitments in Europe and that Japan threatened both. The fall of France in 1940 coincided closely with the Japanese invasion of France's colonies in Southeast Asia. Almost simultaneously, the United States undertook economic sanctions against Japan.

The war itself, at the center of this period, was important in the strategies it created and the breadth of the political change it brought. WWII inaugurated a new era of naval warfare, covering thousands of square miles within a single battle. At first, an area with nearly 100 million people in it was conquered by Japan, only to recede under the naval and land thrusts of the United States across the Pacific.

The nuclear strikes against Japan were the final stage in a death agony that included devastating incendiary raids on its urban centers. The destruction throughout Asia that resulted from the war left a power vacuum into which the United States was inexorably drawn. The success of the Allied Occupation of Japan set the stage for its later economic successes. The Japanese were astute, devoted students of the United States, and their energies and business practices were such that they eventually surpassed their teachers. The basis of this success is often traced to the Occupation, and in many respects that era can be seen as a watershed in contemporary Japanese history, but the foundation of the Japanese "miracle" was laid decades and even centuries earlier in the development of a culture that accepted intense competition alongside a hierarchical social structure, and which invented new capitalist institutions (such as the *zaibatsu*) as early as the Meiji period.

Following the war, from the late 1940s through the 1950s, resurgent nationalist movements succeeded in establishing new governments. The transition to independence was turbulent and occasionally violent. In Vietnam, politics quickly polarized between a French regime and a communist-led nationalist movement under Ho Chi Minh. Indonesia prevailed against the Dutch under the leadership of Sukarno. In the

Philippines, the transition to democracy was at last complete, but its promising beginnings were stunted by the accidental death of its early champion and charismatic president, Ramon Magsaysay.

STUDY RESOURCES

Video: "Writers and Revolutionaries"
Text: Chapter 5: *Maelstrom: The Pacific War and Its Aftermath*
Review: Chapter 4: Sections on Kita Ikki and Lu Xun.

STUDY FOCUS

After viewing the video and reading Chapter 5, you should have a basic understanding of the following concepts.

1. Global circumstances that led to the US decision to impose an embargo on Japan, and Japan's response to the embargo.

2. The location and impact of the sea and air war in the Pacific Theater of WWII.

3. The original location and significance of Japan's invasions of East and Southeast Asia, and the postwar effects in those areas.

4. The impact of the Cold War on intra-regional relationships immediately after WWII.

5. The fact that WWII was a catalyst for nationalist movements in Pacific Asia.

KEY CONCEPTS AND NAMES

This is a list of important terms, people, and places that you should understand from reading the text. If you cannot think of a brief explanation for everything on this list, you need to read the text again.

Article Nine
Bandung Conference
Democratic Republic of Vietnam
Dien Bien Phu
French Indochina
Greater East Asia Co-prosperity
  Sphere
Hiroshima
Hukbalahap
Kita Ikki

Lu Xun
Douglas MacArthur
Nagasaki
Occupation
Pearl Harbor
Pemuda
SCAP
Showa Emperor (Hirohito)
Viet Minh
World War II

GLOSSARY

■ **General**

Allies: Also known as the Allied powers. The victors of WWII, namely, China, France, the UK, the USA, and the USSR. This alliance came about as a response to the Axis of the Tripartite Pact. These countries are also the permanent members of the UN Security Council; this is a direct result of this wartime marriage of convenience.

Axis: Also known as the Axis powers. The vanquished of WWII, namely, Germany, Italy, and Japan. The Axis countries were those that signed the Tripartite Pact.

Bandung Conference: In response to the growing polarization of international politics in the postwar period, a group of Asian countries --India, Burma, Indonesia, Pakistan, and Ceylon (now Sri Lanka)-- invited the PRC to attend the first meeting of non-aligned countries. This conference was held in Bandung, Indonesia, in the spring of 1955. In all, twenty-nine African and Asian countries (comprising what came to be known as the "Third World") attended. Among those attending the conference were China's Zhou Enlai, India's Nehru, Indonesia's Sukarno, and Egypt's Nasser.

British Malaya: A former British colony in Southeast Asia, developed from what had been the Straits Settlements in modern Malaysia, was formed from parts of Malaya, British Borneo, and Sarawak after

WWII. Singapore was part of both British Malaya and Malaysia, until it became an independent state in 1965.

Ethnocentrism: The belief that one's ethnic or cultural group is superior to others. Race or culture is the central consideration. Examples include the following: the Western attitude toward Asia (e.g., the American attitude toward Japan during the Occupation); the traditional Chinese attitude to all non-Chinese peoples; the French attitude toward the English; and the Japanese attitude toward other Asians.

Douglas MacArthur: 1880-1964. After graduating first in the West Point class of 1903, Douglas MacArthur went on tours of duty in the Philippines and Japan, then to WWI Europe. Later, he became the chief military advisor to the Philippines.

In July 1941, MacArthur was appointed commander of US forces in the Far East. During the war, MacArthur's greatest achievement was the island-hopping counterattack in New Guinea and the Philippines. MacArthur accepted the Japanese surrender on board the USS Missouri on 2 September 1945.

Presiding over the reshaping and democratization of postwar Japan as Supreme Commander of Allied Powers (SCAP), MacArthur implemented numerous reforms, including the new constitution.

In 1950, when the Korean War erupted, MacArthur commanded the UN forces in Korea. MacArthur's proposed strategy was to expand the war and attack China; Truman wanted the war limited to Korea. President Truman prevailed, relieving MacArthur of command in 1951. This was MacArthur's final "lesson in democracy" for Japan--civilian authority is more important than military authority.

SCAP: Supreme Commander for the Allied Powers, namely, General Douglas MacArthur.

Tripartite Pact: Signed in September 1940 by Germany, Italy, and Japan, this military alliance was primarily a marriage of convenience for Japan. However, it further influenced Allied opinion against Japan.

■ <u>China</u>

Lu Xun: (loo shun) Pen name of Zhou Shuren, 1881-1936. He went to Japan to study medicine, but switched to literature after deciding he could best help China by writing. He was China's strongest proponent of language reform. His most famous works, *Diary of a Madman* and *The True Story of Ah Q*, attacked the very soul of traditional China and dismissed the Xinhai Revolution as meaningless. Although not a communist, Lu Xun is hailed by the CCP as the premier leftist writer.

■ Indonesia

Diplomasi: A program to negotiate with the Dutch for independence during the Indonesian revolution.

Pemuda: (peh moo duh) Literally, "youth." Refers to the young who participated in, and were instrumental to, the Indonesian revolution.

Republic of Indonesia: Taking advantage of Japan's defeat and the absence of the Dutch, Sukarno and Mohammed Hatta proclaimed an independent Republic on 17 August 1945. The Dutch, with the aid of the British, tried to re-establish control. However, Holland ultimately granted independence to its former colony on 27 December 1949.

■ Japan

Article Nine: The article in the postwar "peace constitution" which forbids Japanese rearmament. It reads as follows:

> *Article 9. Aspiring sincerely to an international peace based on justice and order, the Japanese people forever renounce war as a sovereign right of the nation and the threat or use of force as means of settling international disputes.*
>
> *(2) In order to accomplish the aim of the preceding paragraph, land, sea, and air forces, as well as other war potential, will never be maintained. The right of belligerency of the state will not be recognized.*

In spite of the seemingly clear wording of Article Nine, Japan has created what it calls its Self Defense Forces (SDF). The debate over the legality of the SDF has gone on since the SDF were formed. The ultimate conclusion is that war in self-defense is not forbidden, so defensive armament is constitutional.

Public opinion polls consistently show the majority of the Japanese people are against any amendment to Article Nine which might increase armament. Such polls also show that most Japanese favor maintaining the SDF, regardless of the possible unconstitutionality of the SDF's existence.

Greater East Asia Co-prosperity Sphere: A wartime slogan used by the Japanese government to promote a politically and economically unified Asia, led by Japan and free from Western influence. The "members" of the sphere were Japan, China, Manchukuo, French Indochina, and the Dutch East Indies. Although the sphere was primarily a justification for Japanese expansion, some hailed the sphere as a counter to Western imperialism in Asia and as a means to restore control of Asia to Asians.

Others said that it was an excuse to defend Japanese imperialism in Asia. In any case, the idea of an Asia ruled by Asians undoubtedly influenced subsequent nationalist movements in the region.

Hiroshima: (he roe she ma) On 6 August 1945, the world's first atomic bomb was dropped on Hiroshima, demolishing about 90% of the city and ultimately killing some 200,000 people. Peace Memorial Park and related buildings are now at what was the epicenter of the explosion. Every year there is a commemorative ceremony on August 6.

Kita Ikki: (key tah eek key) 1883-1937. A radical writer, fervent nationalist, and extreme socialist. He is sometimes called the father of Japanese fascism. Kita advocated expulsion of the West from Asia by a revolutionary Japanese empire. He wrote several extreme texts, many of which were banned or censored in Japan. He developed a following among young officers, some of whom led the February 26 Incident. Although Kita was not directly involved, he was found guilty of inciting the Incident and executed.

Konoe Fumimaro: (co no eh foo me ma roe) 1891-1945. Konoe advocated Asian self-determination and opposed Western involvement in Asia. Prime minister in 1937-1939 and 1940-1941, his first cabinet presided over the opening of the Sino-Japanese war of 1937-1945; his second cabinet inaugurated the Greater East Asia Co-prosperity Sphere.

Vice prime minister in the first postwar cabinet, Konoe worked for a new Japanese constitution. However, he was indicted as a war criminal. On the day he was to report to Occupation authorities for detention and trial, he committed suicide.

Nagasaki: (nah gah sah key) On 9 August 1945, an atomic bomb was dropped on Nagasaki, where Nagasaki Shipyards was located. About 122,000 people were killed, and most of the city was destroyed. The site of foreign trade before and during the Edo period, Nagasaki is once again a center for shipbuilding. It is also noted for historic Western residences and as a deep-sea port.

Showa Emperor: (show wah) 1902-1989; regent from 1921; reigned 1926-1989. Better known in the West by his given name of Hirohito.

An avid marine biologist whose studies made contributions to the advance of science, the Showa Emperor claimed disinterest in politics. However, it is widely agreed that he played a pivotal role in both the suppression of the February 26 Incident and the decision to surrender in 1945. What role he had in the militarism of the 1930s and 1940s is debated. He said that as a constitutional monarch, all he could do was approve the legislation presented before him, as was required by law--

his opinion was irrelevant. On the other hand, there are those who see a more active wartime role for him.

In the postwar period, the Showa Emperor became the first reigning Japanese emperor to travel abroad. He also visited every Japanese prefecture except Okinawa (for safety reasons). He died of cancer on 7 January 1989.

■ Philippines

Hukbalahap: (who-k bah lah hop) The People's Anti-Japanese Army; also known as the Huks. "Huk" comes from Tagalog "hukbo" (army). The Huks combined peasant agrarian reformers with WWII nationalists into a postwar rebellion (1946-1952) against the Philippine elite. The Huks' association with Philippine Communists drew American attention and resulted in increased aid to Ramon Magsaysay, who broke the guerrilla movement in 1953.

Ramon Magsaysay: (mahg sigh sigh) 1907-1957. President of the Philippines from 1953 until his untimely death in a plane crash, Magsaysay represented the common people. His accomplishments included ending the Huk rebellion, working for major reforms in land distribution and political institutions, and encouraging bright young reformers from commoner background. See Chapter 9.

Tao: (tah' oh) Literally, "man." Refers to Philippine peasants.

■ Vietnam

Bao Dai: (bao dye) Born 1914; reigned 1926-1945. Last emperor of the Vietnamese Nguyen dynasty (1802-1945).

Democratic Republic of Vietnam: (DRV) Established by Ho Chi Minh in Hanoi on 2 September 1945.

The Japanese invaded Vietnam on 9 March 1945, ousting the French. With the defeat of the Japanese in August, the Viet Minh moved into the power void thus created, ended colonial rule, and abolished the traditional monarchy. However, the French tried to retake their old colony. Thirty years of war later, Vietnam was finally unified under Vietnamese (not foreign) rule. See Chapters 9, 11.

Dien Bien Phu: The site of a decisive battle in Vietnam's war against the French (1945-1954).

The French planned to use Dien Bien Phu as a base for disrupting Viet Minh operations in Laos, and poured 11,000 troops into their fortifications there. General Vo Nguyen Giap took advantage of this troop concentration and delivered a powerful blow to French forces. After surrounding the French base with his troops and heavy artillery, Giap launched an assault on 13 March 1954. The fighting favored the Viet Minh, and on 7 May, the French headquarters was taken. With more than 10,000 prisoners in Viet Minh hands, the French conceded defeat in their attempt to control Vietnam.

Vo Nguyen Giap: (voe win yahp) Born 1910. Active in communist organizations since the early 1930s, Vo Nguyen Giap rose in party ranks during WWII and was chosen by Ho Chi Minh to command the Vietnamese Liberation Army. His ideas on "people's war" became the strategy which ousted the French (and later, the Americans) from Vietnam. In the 1980s, Vo Nguyen Giap's importance waned, and in 1982, he lost his seat on the Politburo. See Chapter 11.

TIME-FRAME QUESTIONS

1. a. Death of Sun Yat-sen.
   b. Execution of Jose Rizal.
   c. Death of Lu Xun.
   d. Execution of Kita Ikki.
   e. Death of Taisho Emperor.

2. a. Outbreak of war in Europe.
   b. Sneak attack on Pearl Harbor.
   c. Establishment of Manchukuo.
   d. Japanese invasion of French Indochina.
   e. The Mukden Incident.

3. a. Russo-Japanese Nonaggression Pact.
   b. Signing of the Tripartite Pact.
   c. Notice given ending Japanese-American Commercial Treaty.
   d. German-Japanese Alliance.
   e. Reopening of the war in China.

4. a. Greater East Asia Co-prosperity Sphere Conference.
   b. Liberation of Guam.
   c. The Battle of Midway.
   d. Closure of the Burma Road.
   e. Soviet armies overrun Manchuria.

5. a. Death of Ramon Magsaysay.
    b. Bandung Conference.
    c. Sukarno and Hatta proclaim Indonesian independence.
    d. Ho Chi Minh declares Vietnamese independence.
    e. Geneva Agreement on Vietnam.

6. a. Atomic bomb dropped on Nagasaki.
    b. Signing of documents on the USS Missouri.
    c. Establishment of the People's Republic of China.
    d. Atomic bomb dropped on Hiroshima.
    e. Defeat of Germany.

7. a. Dutch launch "Police Action" in Indonesia.
    b. Magsaysay elected president of the Philippines.
    c. Fall of Vichy France.
    d. Amnesty for collaborators announced in Philippines.
    e. Japan surrenders to Allies.

8. a. Truman dismisses MacArthur.
    b. The Chinese enter the Korean War.
    c. Jacob Malik, UN delegate from the USSR, calls for armistice.
    d. MacArthur's forces take Pyongyang.
    e. Syngman Rhee boasts that the South can take Pyongyang in three days.

QUESTIONS FOR REVIEW

1. What was the importance of literature and writing to Asian political movements of the early twentieth century? Who were the most prominent authors? (Think back to the video.)

2. What influence, if any, did the military have on Japanese politics in the pre–WWII period? Why was Kita Ikki influential with certain young officers? What did he accomplish? How?

3. Look at the list of Key Concepts and Names for this chapter. Find all place names, then locate each place on the maps in the text.

4. Who was Ramon Magsaysay? What did he accomplish?

5. What were the terms and goals of the 1954 Geneva Agreement? Which terms were carried out? Which were not? How? Why?

6. What was the purpose of the 1955 Bandung Conference? What nations sent representatives? What precepts were spelled out?

7. Zhou Enlai made expert diplomatic maneuvers at the Bandung Conference. What were his statements, proposals, and achievements? Did Zhou have a lasting impact? If so, what was it?

8. Both the Dutch and the French tried to re-establish control of their Asian colonies after WWII. How did other Western powers help or hinder these attempts?

9. Although the sneak attack on Pearl Harbor was a brilliant military success, it was a tactical mistake. Why? What were the goals of the attack on Pearl Harbor? Were they achieved?

10. What was the impact of the Japanese occupation of Indonesia on Indonesian nationalism? How was postwar Indonesia different from the prewar Indonesia the Dutch had known?

11. How useful was the Tripartite Pact to the Japanese? Why would a non-fascist government ally itself with fascist states? How did this alliance affect Anglo-American views of Japan?

12. Characterize the national mood of Japan in the 1930s. Did it differ from the national mood of Meiji Japan? How?

13. How open were Japanese politics in the 1920s? the 1930s? the 1940s? What forces were at work to change the openness of Japanese politics?

14. Who fought the Battle of Dien Bien Phu? One side was stunningly defeated. Which? What were the consequences of the battle?

ADDITIONAL RECOMMENDED READINGS

Hersey, John. *Hiroshima*. New York: Alfred A. Knopf, 1946.

Ienaga, Saburo. *The Pacific War, 1931-1945*. New York: Pantheon Books, 1978.

Iriye, Akira and Warren Cohen, eds. *American, Chinese, and Japanese Perspectives on Wartime Asia*. Wilmington: Scholarly Resources, 1990.

Keene, Donald, ed. *Modern Japanese Literature*. New York: Grove Press, Inc., 1956.

Kervliet, Benedict J. *The Huk Rebellion: A Study of Peasant Revolt in the Philippines*. Berkeley: University of California Press, 1977.

Lu Xun. *Silent China*. London: Oxford University Press, 1973. Edited and tr. by Gladys Yang.

Reid, A.J.S. *Indonesia Nationalist Revolution, 1945-1950*. Melbourne: Longmans, 1974.

UNIT SIX

Post–WWII Asia:
Reinventing Japan, Redividing Korea

OVERVIEW

Perhaps no period in the American interaction with a single Asian nation was so infused with a sense of "mission" as the Occupation of Japan. The occupiers moved into the Shibuya area of Tokyo, created a middle class suburb called Washington Heights, and set about what they saw as the task of dismantling feudal Japan and bringing American democracy to Japan.

The video treatment of the American Occupation of Japan provides an opportunity to raise questions about the malleability of the Japanese during this period and the extent to which they used the American presence to enact changes that would strengthen their economy. It is useful to stress how stunned and astonished the Japanese were, at first, by the total ease and confidence the Americans exuded, in their manner, their actions, even in the way they walked. It was almost as though the Americans were unaware of what they had done--they had defeated a country that had never lost a war, they set foot on the homeland where no foreigner had tread except by Japanese will. The Japanese were in awe of these conquerors and the nonchalance with which they wielded their power, and thus were unusually (although not entirely) open to accepting whatever the Occupation might propose.

In newsreel fashion, the video segment in this unit chronicles the personnel and agency of SCAP (Supreme Commander of the Allied Powers). Bright, young New-Dealers arrived in Japan to do what their college classmates did under Roosevelt in the United States. The occupiers moved into Tokyo and set about what they saw as the task of dismantling feudal Japan and introducing it to American democracy.

In the video, we hear from some of those who were in SCAP during the Occupation. Even forty years later, they are both embarrassed at the degree of their interference in the governance of a foreign country, and a little amazed at what they were able to accomplish, from labor laws to tax reforms. These were social and economic changes more radical than anything they would have been able to accomplish in America. The imperious and aloof MacArthur was undisturbed by his own paternalism, as reflected in his famous photograph alongside the Showa Emperor.

The occupation of Korea was an altogether different matter. It occurred almost as an afterthought in American postwar planning: the US 24th Corps in Okinawa was directed at the last minute to take charge in Korea after having prepared to participate in the Japanese occupation. The initial rationale for the occupation of Korea was merely as a buffer for *Japan*. The latter country was seen as a vital component of America's strategic interests in the Asia-Pacific region, but not Korea. American leaders, including General Douglas MacArthur, made statements in 1946-47 that Korea was not a vital strategic interest of the United States. Nor did Americans understand the deep divisions that had been developing in Korean society over the previous decades. For these reasons, the military command assigned to Korea was especially ill-prepared to take charge there. Americans in Korea were no less determined than their counterparts in Japan to establish the foundations for a new society oriented toward American-style democracy and capitalism, yet the United States was much more eager to rid itself of the burden of occupying Korea than Japan. The formal occupation of Korea ended in 1949; the occupation of Japan ended in 1952.

In other respects, there were strong parallels between the two occupations. In both there was a split between the American occupiers "in country" and their superiors in Washington. In country, the leaders of the occupation strove to promote US interests from the perspective of mostly internal, domestic political factors, while across the Pacific in Washington, leaders were governed by the perspective of a great power with global interests. The result was a clash of viewpoints that, in the case of Japan, altered the occupiers' original blueprint. The occupation policy in Japan was modified to stimulate faster growth and shore up the country politically and economically as a bulwark against Soviet expansionism in Asia. In Korea, however, events on the ground overwhelmed the best intentions of the "internationalist" planners in Washington who sought eventually to re-unite the country.

In some respects, Korea was a divided nation before the imposition of the arbitrary line in 1945 that separates the two halves of the peninsula today. As noted in Chapter 4, millions of Koreans were taken by force or circumstance to work abroad in the factories and camps of the Japanese empire, a massive dislocation that was still in the process of adjustment when the Korean War broke out. Politically, the country was divided between tenants and landlords, Left and Right wing political factions. Carter Eckert emphasizes this in the text: "long before any artificial geographic lines had been drawn at the thirty-eighth parallel, Korea was already an ideologically bifurcated society."

A great tragedy for Koreans that did not resolve their national dilemma, the Korean War nonetheless had a powerful stimulative effect in Japan and virtually saved it from economic collapse under the severe policies that had been imposed by Joseph Dodge. Korea and Japan became linked strategically in the minds of American planners following the Korean War, and this profoundly affected the tolerance by Americans of protectionism in both countries during the early postwar period. The "re-occupation" of Korea in order to save it from the invasion by the north not only militarized the American policy of containment worldwide, it militarized the bilateral relationship with Korea in ways that never applied in Japan. Korea could be encouraged to re-arm as a military ally; Japan resisted a drastic rearmament and its neighbors concurred. A mutual defense treaty was signed between the United States and Korea in 1953. The mutual defense treaty was made permanent with Japan in 1960 amid violent left-wing protests.

The forging of postwar relationships with Japan and Korea against a background of Cold War rivalry with the Soviet Union profoundly shaped the decades to follow in the Pacific Basin. The two allies became staging points and arsenals of the future conflict in Vietnam. Korea sent thousands of its own troops to fight in Vietnam alongside the Americans. The two American occupations in East Asia were, ultimately, an effort to assert through direct controls the validity of the American Revolution and the New Deal as opposed to the Russian Revolution and the Soviet New Man.

The occupation forces in Japan and Korea sought to mold each society to fit an American model, but they succeeded only very partially in doing so. Nevertheless, the assurance of the American security umbrella and the shoring up of their orientations toward democracy and capitalism started Japan and Korea on their paths toward stability and spectacular economic recoveries.

STUDY RESOURCES

Video: "Reinventing Japan"

Text: Chapter 5: *Maelstrom: The Pacific War and Its Aftermath* (review sections on the American Occupation of Japan); Chapter 6: *Miracle by Design: Postwar Resurgence of Japan* (read the introductory sections up to "Post-Occupation Policies"); and Chapter 9: *Sentimental Imperialists: Americans in Asia* (read "Korea: Liberation, Division, and War, 1945-53").

Note: Unit 6 provides an opportunity to examine the impact of the American Occupations of Japan and Korea after World War II and their influence on early postwar changes in East Asia. To do so, the student should: first, review the section on the American Occupation of Japan in Chapter 5; second, read the introductory sections of Chapter 6; and third, read the Korea section of Chapter 9, as noted above. In conjunction with this reading, the student should view the television segment which focuses on the American Occupation of Japan.

STUDY FOCUS

After viewing the video and reading sections of Chapters 6 and 9, and reviewing Chapter 5, you should have a basic understanding of the following concepts.

1. The changes imposed on all aspects of Japanese society by the Occupation.

2. The origins of the Korean War and its immediate and long term affect on US policy toward Communist Asia.

3. The assurance of the American security umbrella stabilized Japan and Korea, and started each on a path toward spectacular economic recovery.

4. The complex role the Cold War has played in the post–WWII evolution of regional relationships in Pacific Asia.

KEY CONCEPTS AND NAMES

This is a list of important terms, people, and places that you should understand from reading the text. If you cannot think of a brief explanation for everything on this list, you need to read the text again.

Article Nine	ROK
Joseph Dodge	SCAP
Kim Il Sung	Showa Emperor (Hirohito)
KPR	Syngman Rhee
Douglas MacArthur	USAMGIK
Nissan Strike	World War II
Occupation	

GLOSSARY

■ General

Douglas MacArthur: See Unit Five.

San Francisco Peace Treaty: Signed on 8 September 1951 and ratified in April 1952, it ended the Occupation, renounced Japan's claims to all territories acquired after 1895, and gave Japan the leeway it needed to rebuild its economy. This re-establishment of Japanese sovereignty was the high point of Yoshida's diplomatic career.

■ Japan

Article Nine: See Unit Five.

Diet: The Japanese parliament.

SCAP: Supreme Commander for the Allied Powers, namely, General Douglas MacArthur.

Showa Emperor: See Unit Five.

■ Korea

Choson Inmin Konghwaguk: (choe son in min kohng hwah gook) Korean for Korean Peoples' Republic.

DPRK: Acronym for Democratic Peoples' Republic of Korea; commonly called North Korea.

Kim Il Sung: (kim ill soong) Born Kim Song-ju in 1912, Kim has been the sole leader of the Democratic People's Republic of Korea since its founding in September 1948. Under Kim's direction, North Korea has become isolated from the outside world, even within the Soviet bloc.

Korean War: A confrontation between the Republic of Korea (ROK), the US, and the UN on one side, and the Democratic People's Republic of Korea (DPRK), the Soviet Union, and the PRC on the other. The official dates for the war are 25 June 1950 to 27 July 1953. From the Korean point of view, however, the conflict started immediately after the end of WWII, when Korea was divided into American- and Soviet-occupied zones, and lasts to this day; the ROK never signed the armistice which ended the armed hostilities. The demilitarized zone between the Koreas is one of the most heavily armed borders in the world.

At the end of WWII, Korea was split at the thirty-eighth parallel--an artificial division imposed by outside powers. Although the UN tried to unify the peninsula and sponsored elections in 1948, the Soviets denied UN representatives access to North Korea. In June 1950, the North invaded the South, and pushed the ROK forces back to a small corner in the Southeast. The MacArthur-led forces of the South launched an offensive in September, and pushed up to the Yalu River (Amnok-kang), the border with China. The PRC, feeling threatened by the proximity of enemy armies, entered the war at this point, repulsing the forces of the South. Eventually, the North worked its way back to the thirty-eighth parallel--back to where the war started. Armistice negotiations began in mid-1951 and dragged on for two years. Approximately four million people died in a war that changed no borders.

The Korean War's greatest significance for Japan was as a catalyst for economic revival and growth. It also changed the US approach to Japan--from reform of an old enemy to reconstruction of a new ally.

KPR: Acronym for Korean Peoples' Republic, the state founded on 6 September 1945.

NKPA: Acronym for North Korean People's Army. The army which invaded South Korea in 1950.

QUESTIONS FOR REVIEW

1. What were the goals of the Occupation? Were these goals achieved?

2. The Occupation forced many political, economic, and even societal changes upon Japan. Name as many as you can.

3. The American Occupation of Japan has been termed an "imported revolution." What is the reasoning behind use of the term "revolution?" What aspects of postwar changes were "imported?" Why? What made postwar democratization so different from Japan's prewar parliamentary experiences?

4. Although not directly involved, Japan was affected by the Korean War (1950-53). What were the effects of the Korean War on Japan and its economy?

5. The Korean War began and ended with the thirty-eighth parallel serving as the division between the North and the South. With this result in mind, how would you describe the outcome of the war? Was it

a victory or a defeat for either side? What importance, if any, do you think the Korean War had in US history? in East Asian history? to international relations?

6. In what ways can Kim Il Sung be compared to the Yi rulers of Korea who shut their country off from the outside world?

ADDITIONAL RECOMMENDED READINGS

Cumings, Bruce. *The Origins of the Korean War: Liberation and the Emergence of Separate Regimes, 1945-47.* Princeton, NJ: Princeton University Press, 1981.

Kawai, Kazuo. *Japan's American Interlude.* Chicago, IL: University of Chicago Press, 1960.

Reischauer, Edwin O. *The Japanese Today.* Cambridge: Harvard University Press, 1988.

Schaler, Michael. *The American Occupation of Japan.* London: Oxford University Press, 1985.

Suh, Kuk-sung, et al., eds. *The Identity of the Korean People: A History of Legitimacy on the Korean Peninsula.* Seoul: Research Center for Peace and Reunification, 1983.

UNIT SEVEN

Miracle by Design: The Postwar Resurgence of Japan

OVERVIEW

With the war behind them, the Japanese set out on a grand scale to become viable world traders. In the early 1960s, Prime Minister Ikeda Hayato, supported by a group of extraordinarily far-seeing bureaucrats and young aggressive business managers, set out to redirect Japan's energies from the ideological bickering of the postwar period into a single-minded pursuit of economic gain. Ikeda's "Double Your Income" policy was to help build up a new industrial structure for Japan. Its success was fueled by heavy capital investment at the disposal of the government's financial planners--made possible by high personal savings and a banking apparatus adapted to Japan's needs.

The acquisitive instincts unleashed in this burst of activity were corporate and group-directed rather than individual, though Japan does have its quota of individual entrepreneurs. The authoritarianism and group/national identity which the Tokugawa used to fortify their shogunate in the Edo period unexpectedly served as an adhesive linking the different and often disparate elements of Japan's modern-day business society. If the average Japanese businessman of today knows little about the power structure of the Tokugawa *bakufu*, he nevertheless exhibits aspects of that tradition in his daily life.

This unit shows how the Japanese, in the wake of their WWII disasters, made business history through a combination of international marketing, technological improvements, labor-management harmony, and a keen sense of international business competition honed on fierce domestic competition. Japan's economic success was not based merely on business skills and cultural factors; the success was also supported by the "development economy" of a skilled bureaucracy working in the Meiji tradition. Through such organizations as the Economic Planning Agency and the redoubtable Ministry for International Trade and Industry (MITI), not to mention the Ministry of Finance and the Bank of Japan, government planners set the beat for Japan's sudden rise in productivity and business efficiency.

Yet beyond all these important factors, the real leaders of the economic surge were a new generation of business managers. By looking at the international marketing work of such companies as Sony, Matsushita (Panasonic), Toyota, Honda, and latter day successes like Fujitsu and Kyocera, we can chart the rise in Japan's GNP. The trading companies, exemplified by Mitsubishi and Mitsui, deserve attention as extraordinary world marketing influences.

In the video for this unit, we enter the Japanese factories, see the people who work there and how they work, while voice-overs and interviews with Japanese experts offer a cross-section of views about how their successes have been achieved. Businessmen, bankers, and bureaucrats provide insights into the distinctive kind of management-labor relationship that has been constructed, and the relatively small gap--amazingly small by US standards--between the compensation and living standards of top Japanese executives and the average workers.

STUDY RESOURCES

Video: "Inside Japan Inc. "
Text: Chapter 6: *Miracle by Design: The Postwar Resurgence of Japan*

STUDY FOCUS

After viewing the video and reading Chapter 6, you should have a basic understanding of the following concepts.

1. The importance of government planning in Japan's economic success.

2. The impact of young executives and bureaucrats who planned for long-range goals.

3. The significance of Japan's labor-management relationship and how the relationship developed.

4. The reform of the Japanese economy imposed by the US-led Occupation, particularly the transition from *zaibatsu* to *keiretsu*, and how these developments affected economic growth.

5. Japan's trade dependency, and vulnerability, with respect to energy and food imports.

6. The debate over Japan's proper role on the international stage.

KEY CONCEPTS AND NAMES

This is a list of important terms and people that you should understand from reading the text. If you cannot think of a brief explanation for everything on this list, you need to read the text again.

Capitalist Developmental State   MITI
Joseph Dodge   Nakasone Yasuhiro
Keiretsu   Nissan Strike
LDP   OPEC
Lifetime Employment   Technology Transfers
Maekawa Report   Yoshida Shigeru/Yoshida Doctrine
Market Rational/Plan Rational   *Zoku*

GLOSSARY

■ **General**

GNP: Gross National Product. The total of goods and services produced by a given country.

Information Society: An inter-related world economy based on modern technology, such as computers, facsimiles, and shared data bases. The emphasis is on intangibles, not physical products and facilities.

Market Rational/Plan Rational: Both terms refer to economic systems. A market rational economy reflects any changes in the basic market forces (i.e., supply and demand), and has limited governmental regulation. A plan rational economy reflects the formulation and implementation of an economic policy, and close cooperation between business and government. The US has a market rational economy and Japan has a plan rational economy.

Multinational Corporation: A company which operates in several countries, e.g., AT&T, Blaupunkt, Guiness, Honda, IBM, Mitsubishi, Phillips Electronics, Volkswagen, and Volvo.

Nixon Shocks: In 1971, President Richard Nixon implemented several policy changes which strongly affected Japan, including a 10% surcharge on Japanese imports, a halt to US soybean exports to Japan, and normalization of relations with the PRC.

Oil Crisis: OPEC's use of oil supplies as a political weapon against industrialized countries. The first oil crisis was 1973-74, and the second was 1979-80. Both reflected political unrest in the Middle East.

Pax Americana: Latin for "American Peace." A unipolar world system characterized by a lack of conflict and dominance by American military strength. Fashioned after the term "Pax Britannica."

San Francisco Peace Treaty: Signed on 8 September 1951 and ratified in April 1952, it ended the Occupation, renounced Japan's claims to all territories acquired after 1895, and gave Japan the leeway it needed to rebuild its economy. This re-establishment of Japanese sovereignty was the high point of Yoshida's diplomatic career.

Stagflation: A combination of the words "stagnation" and "inflation." An economic situation in which growth is negligible (i.e., stagnant) and expenditures increase faster than income (i.e., inflation). Stagflation describes the US economy during parts of the mid- and late 1970s.

Trade Surplus/Trade Deficit: The most comprehensive measure of a trade surplus or deficit is the current account balance, which is the difference between the exports of all goods and services and the imports of the same.

■ Japan

Diet: The Japanese parliament.

Japan, Inc.: The perception of Japan as a monolith of business and government working in tandem.

Keiretsu: (kay reh tsoo) Japanese corporate alliances typically affiliated with a bank and a trading company. The member companies own significant parts of each other.

LDP: Liberal Democratic Party. Formed in 1955, the LDP and its predecessors have held power in Japan almost continuously since the end of the war. A conservative party, the LDP is supported by the powerful farm lobby and big business.

Lifetime Employment: A system which treats employees as human capital, rather than as business expenses. For example, when a job is eliminated, the employee is not fired. Instead, the employee is retrained for another position within the same company. However, this system only applies to the largest corporations, and primarily to male white-collar workers. Other workers "pay" for the lifetime employment of others by being underpaid and expendable.

Maekawa Report: (mah eh caw wah) A report released by the Advisory Group on Economic Structural Adjustment in April 1986. Named for Maekawa Haruhiko, the group's chairman, the report advocated changing Japan's economic structure to better harmonize with that of the world economy. These are the report's five proposals:

1. Stimulate domestic demand;
2. Change industrial structure to contribute to world harmony;
3. Improve access to Japanese markets and stimulate imports;
4. Stabilize international exchange rates and liberalize international financial markets;
5. Contribute internationally at a level appropriate to Japan's status.

The government accepted these proposals, and then-Prime Minister Nakasone headed a Task Force on Economic Structural Adjustment to implement these recommendations.

MITI: The Ministry of International Trade and Industry. MITI is the government agency which promotes cooperative planning between business and government. Widely regarded, both domestically and internationally, as the basic promoter of a highly successful policy of expanding Japanese business interests in the world free market, MITI's direct influence over businesses has declined somewhat since the 1970s.

Nakasone Yasuhiro: (nah caw so neh yah sue he roe) Born 1918. Elected to the House of Representatives in 1947, he has been reelected in every subsequent election. His unusual political style keeps him in the spotlight rather than the sidelines. Head of his own faction in the LDP, Nakasone became prime minister in 1982. He held that post for a surprisingly long time in Japanese politics--5 years--before he was finally forced to resign. His successor was Takeshita Noboru. Nakasone was a key player in the Recruit scandal of the late 1980s which rocked the LDP. He resigned from the LDP and his own faction in May 1989, but he retained his seat in the Diet and was reelected later that year.

Non-Nuclear Policy: Japan's non-nuclear policy is as follows:

1. Reliance on the US nuclear umbrella for protection.
2. The three non-nuclear principles.
3. Promotion of world-wide disarmament.
4. Peaceful development of nuclear energy.

This policy has allowed Japan to take a stance in world affairs independent of the arms race.

Non-Nuclear Principles: These are the non-nuclear principles of Japan:

1. No Japanese production of nuclear weapons.
2. No possession of nuclear weapons by the Japanese government.
3. No introduction of nuclear weapons into Japanese territory.

SDPJ: Acronym for the Social Democratic Party of Japan. Formerly known as the Japan Socialist Party (JSP); also known as the socialists.

Self Defense Forces: Although Article Nine of the 1947 Constitution forbids Japan from making war as a means to resolve international conflicts, it does not expressly forbid self defense. It is from this point of view that Japan has created its Self Defense Forces (SDF).

Starting with the MacArthur-ordered establishment of a National Police Reserve in 1950, Japan's defensive capability has grown, partly in response to Cold War tensions (particularly those in Korea), and partly in response to American urging (primarily by John Foster Dulles, US Secretary of State from 1953 to 1959). In 1954, the Self Defense Forces Law was enacted, and the Self Defense Forces (SDF) acquired their present name. The SDF may be mobilized in the event of threat or attack from abroad, civil unrest, threat to Japanese airspace or territorial waters, and in response to natural disasters. Uniformed members of the SDF are permitted to bear arms.

In 1976, Japanese lawmakers instituted a policy to limit defense spending to 1% of the GNP. However, defense spending broke the 1% "barrier" in the 1980s, causing domestic furor. (Still, defense spending came nowhere near 2% of Japan's GNP.) Even though Japanese defense spending is a tiny portion of the total budget, Japan was *third* in defense expenditures in the late 1980s, behind the USA and USSR.

There are those who argue that the very existence of the SDF is illegal, as the establishment of armed forces is forbidden by Article Nine. However, the existence of the SDF is a fact, and there is general acceptance by the Japanese people of the validity of the SDF.

Shinkansen: (sheen kahn sehn) Literally, "new trunk line"; the bullet train. A system of super-express passenger trains which connects major Japanese cities, overlaid on top of the existing train system. Used primarily for travel, not freight transport. However, with skyrocketing land prices and rents in the Tokyo area, it is being used more and more for commuting.

Yasukuni Shrine: (yah sue coo knee) Literally, "peaceful country shrine;" also interpreted "shrine for the repose of the nation." A Shinto shrine in the Tokyo area which memorializes all who died in Japanese civil and foreign wars since 1853. Founded in 1869, Yasukuni was initially dedicated to those who died to restore the emperor. In the 1930s, it became a center for "state Shinto," an amalgamation of traditional Shinto beliefs, patriotism, and militarism. Since the mid-1950s, various conservative groups (including the LDP) have tried to reinstate official support for Yasukuni; however, strong opposition has prevented such support.

Yasukuni Shrine is a political hotbed. Then-Prime Minister Ohira Masayoshi made a "private visit" to the shrine in 1979, just months after major war criminals had been enshrined there. Nakasone Yasuhiro paid an official visit to Yasukuni in 1986, while serving as prime minister. Both events caused uproars, both in Japan and abroad.

Yoshida Doctrine: (yo she dah) The term used by some analysts to describe a policy developed by Japanese Prime Minister Yoshida Shigeru, which defined rehabilitation of the Japanese economy as a primary goal. It also advocated a non-military, pacifist role for Japan in international politics, and allowed for US military bases in Japan to provide security.

Yoshida Shigeru: (she geh roo) 1878-1967. Yoshida entered the Foreign Ministry in 1906. He had a distinguished career as a diplomat, serving in various posts around the world. He retired in 1935, but was reinstated to serve as ambassador to Great Britain, his highest post. After being recalled to Japan in 1938, Yoshida held no further official positions.

Since Yoshida had been relatively uninvolved in politics during WWII, Occupation authorities allowed him to serve in the postwar government. He became foreign minister in 1945. Yoshida set up a crucial meeting between the Showa Emperor and MacArthur, after which MacArthur endorsed both the Japanese imperial system and the current monarch.

In April 1946, Yoshida became prime minister. He held that post until October 1954, except a period from May 1947 to October 1948, which was the only time during the postwar period that the LDP (or its predecessors) did not rule.

During his tenure as prime minister, Yoshida accomplished much, including formulating what is known as "the Yoshida Doctrine." Yoshida regarded Japan's return to sovereignty as his greatest achievement. This was attained with the signing of the San Francisco Peace Treaty in September 1951. This treaty gave Japan the leeway it needed to rebuild its economy.

Dissent within Japan led to Yoshida's resignation in October 1954. Nonetheless, many of Yoshida's policies remained in force, contributing to Japan's postwar success. He enjoyed the status of a respected elder statesman until his death in 1967.

Zoku: A "policy tribe" whose members in the Japanese Diet regularly receive campaign contributions from the industry they are supposed to monitor and regulate. There is a *zoku* for nearly every major industry group in Japan.

TIME-FRAME QUESTIONS

1. a. Saddam Hussein orders invasion of Kuwait.
   b. Japan's Foreign Capital Law enacted.
   c. The Plaza Accord.
   d. Second Oil Crisis.
   e. Reagan elected president.

2. a. Dodge Mission to Japan.
   b. Outbreak of Korean War.
   c. MacArthur forbids General Strike.
   d. End of Occupation.
   e. Bandung Conference.

3. a. Signing of San Francisco Peace Treaty.
   b. Thomas Dewey nearly becomes President.
   c. New Japanese Constitution.
   d. Nissan Strike.
   e. Dissolution of Manchukuo.

4. a. Nixon Shocks.
   b. Floating exchange rate for the Yen.
   c. Nakasone Yasuhiro elected prime minister.
   d. Tanaka Kakuei elected prime minister.
   e. US introduces trigger prices for Japanese steel.

QUESTIONS FOR REVIEW

1. What did Yoshida deem to be the "excesses of democracy?" How did he want the government to respond?

2. In the Chapter Annex of Chapter 6, four competing views of Japan's international role are presented. Re-read these views, then argue for and against each of them. Which do you believe (if any)? Why?

3. Japan's Constitution prohibits armed forces, yet Japan has its Self Defense Forces. How and why has this happened?

4. In the mid-1970s, Japanese industry shifted from its traditional emphases to new ones. Which industries declined? Which grew? Why did the emphasis change?

5. Much has been made of Japan's system of so-called "lifetime employment." What does this system actually entail? How does it affect employers' attitudes toward, and treatment of, employees?

6. Name the major differences between prewar and postwar Japanese industry.

7. What is the importance of technology transfers to the Japanese economy? Is this simply a question of benefit to Japan and detriment to the West?

8. Why did the dollar stay strong and the yen weak during the late 1970s and the early 1980s? Why and how did the yen strengthen in the late 1980s?

9. In the text, Chalmers Johnson has proposed four different explanations of "The Japanese Miracle." Re-read that section. Which, if any, of those theories do you believe is true? Why? Argue for your view and against any you believe to be false.

10. What is the significance of Nakasone's visit to the Yasukuni Shrine to Japan? to other Asian nations? What impact did it have internationally? Why?

11. Part of Japan's modern success is attributed to planning for long term gains rather than short term profits. How has this affected the development of Japanese industry? How has this affected US-Japan bilateral relations?

12. Re-read the reference to Kissinger's comments on Japan in the Chapter Annex of Chapter 6. Do you agree with his assessment? Why?

13. What are the differences between the prewar *zaibatsu* and the postwar *keiretsu*? Be specific.

14. Japan's international political stance is strongly tied to its economic success, in that the Japanese do not attach a moral agenda to trade ("value-free diplomacy"). Contrast this to American foreign policy. Discuss in terms of Japan's trade dependency with respect to energy, food, and other raw material imports.

ADDITIONAL RECOMMENDED READINGS

Ellison, Herbert J., ed. *Japan and The Pacific Quadrille*. Boulder: Westview Press, 1987.

94

Gibney, Frank. *Miracle by Design: The Real Reasons Behind Japan's Economic Success.* New York: Times Books, 1982.

Holstein, William J. *The Japanese Power Game: What It Means for America.* New York: Charles Scribner's Sons, 1990.

Johnson, Chalmers. *MITI and the Japanese Miracle.* Stanford: Stanford University Press, 1982.

Reischauer, Edwin O. *The Japanese Today.* Cambridge: Harvard University Press, 1988.

Whiting, Robert. *You Gotta Have Wa: When Two Cultures Collide on the Baseball Diamond.* New York: MacMillan Publishing Company, 1989.

Woronoff, Jon. *Japan's Commercial Empire.* New York, NY: M.E. Sharpe, 1984.

UNIT EIGHT

The New Asian Capitalists

OVERVIEW

The so-called Japanese miracle was of vital importance to the Pacific Century, not only for the wealth it brought to the region (and a new economic resentment evoking wartime memories), but for the creation of a new Asian approach to capitalism. Borrowing technology and some social institutions from the West, and taking a kick-start from the American Occupation, Japan rose from desperate poverty to incredible affluence in 25 years. It was an example which other Asian countries--most notably Korea and the Newly Industrializing Economies (NIEs)--used in their attempts to duplicate Japan's spectacular success.

The ingredients of these economic miracles have been much discussed in pop-business primers and academic texts. The intent of this unit is not to dwell upon the business prowess of Asian entrepreneurs, but to focus on the emergence of a new socio-economic model in Asia which some argue has been significantly aided by cultural and historical factors. If Japan's economic miracle has become the new exemplar, its modified blueprints are spreading to other parts of Pacific Asia. The parallel rise of the Republic of Korea as one of the world's biggest manufacturers and exporters is the prime example. Modeled closely on Japan's successes (just as Japan used American models), Korea built up its industry seemingly overnight. Korean growth figures are the most spectacular in the world. Will Korean conglomerates like Hyundai overtake their Japanese competitors in some sectors? The possibility cannot be ruled out. Working from the same set of national incentives as the Japanese, Koreans made their country a graphic example of NIE development.

The video segment includes a look at Taiwan as a possible example of "Confucian Capitalism," and raises the general question as to the economic role of Confucian traditions in this and other parts of Asia. In fact, "Confucianism" is a modern concept for which there was no exact equivalent in pre-modern Asia. Even the name "Confucius" is a Latinized version of one of the founders of the tradition, Kong Fuzi. Its ideas and practices evolved differently as it spread through other East

Asian societies; its usefulness as either as a secular philosophy or a political ideology to explain economic success and failure is clearly limited. The video includes interviews with some authorities who suggest that the pervasive influence in certain countries of Confucian principles (emphasis on education and familial ties; guidelines for proper and ethical behavior among individuals, placing them in hierarchical relationships; and stressing social harmony) have reinforced national efforts toward economic development.

It is necessary also to look at the darker side of Confucian traditions, particularly as they may have influenced the degree to which Taiwan and Singapore remain uncomfortably authoritarian societies. While the extent of Confucian influence is impossible to measure, there are intriguing indications of its impact in the evolution of family-based business into corporate empires in Japan, Korea, Taiwan and elsewhere. The effort in China to revive Confucian ideals, after their decline and temporary suppression earlier, exemplifies how some Asians themselves seem to accept a vague connection between a Confucian environment and the "economic miracles" in Hong Kong, Singapore and enclaves of the ethnic Chinese throughout the Pacific world. We hear counter-arguments from experts such as Chalmers Johnson, who stress that economic success has grown primarily from skilled bureaucracies which have used business-government relationships in creative ways that make them powerful competitors in the international arena. The question is left for the viewer to judge, albeit with a clearer understanding of its complexity.

STUDY RESOURCES

Video: "Big Business and the Ghost of Confucius"
Text: Chapter 7: *The New Asian Capitalists*

STUDY FOCUS

After viewing the video and reading Chapter 7, you should have a basic understanding of the following concepts.

1.   The aggregate economic growth of Asian-Pacific countries in the past three decades is unsurpassed by any other world region.

2.   By developing a strong export-market orientation, Japan and the NIEs have successfully utilized growing global economic interdependence.

3. The stress on economic development as a primary national goal has been a major factor in postwar Asian-Pacific successes.

4. Political stability and centrist or conservative domestic orientations seem to have been necessary prerequisites for Asian-Pacific high-growth economies.

5. Historical processes and traditional cultures have helped to shape the postwar political economies of the Asian-Pacific countries, both capitalist and socialist.

6. The distribution of economic achievement in the NIEs differs according to resource endowment, trade orientation, and political ideology.

7. Confucianist traditions appear to have exerted a positive influence on economic development in Pacific Asia in spite of the fact that Confucianism was also used to rationalize resistance to modernization, particularly in the nineteenth century. Then, as now, "Confucianism" can be interpreted by governments in ways that support their national political goals.

KEY CONCEPTS AND NAMES

Below is a list of important terms, people, and places that you should understand from reading the text. If you cannot think of a brief definition or explanation for all of these words, you need to read the text again.

ASEAN/ASEAN-4
Capitalism
Chaebol
Confucianism
Entrepot
Export-led Growth
Familyism
GDP/GNP
Hong Kong
Import Substitution
Indonesia
Industrial Infrastructure
Industrialization

Malaysia
NIE
"Overseas" Chinese
Primary Products
Resource-rich (ASEAN countries)
Syngman Rhee
ROK-Japan Normalization
    Treaty
Singapore
Taiwan
Technology Transfers
Thailand
Trade-dependent Economy

Commonly Used Regional Designations and Acronyms
for Selected Asian Countries

ASEAN	Brunei, Indonesia, Malaysia, Philippines, Singapore, Thailand
ASEAN-4	Indonesia, Malaysia, Philippines, Thailand
ASEAN Members of OPEC	Indonesia
East Asian Nations	China, Japan, Mongolia, North Korea, South Korea, Taiwan
Low-Income Southeast Asian Economies	Burma (Myanmar), Cambodia (Kampuchea), Laos, Vietnam
NIEs ("Little Dragons")	Hong Kong, Singapore, South Korea, Taiwan
Oil-Exporting ASEAN States	Brunei, Indonesia, Malaysia
Oil-Importing ASEAN States	Philippines, Singapore, Thailand
Resource-Rich Nations	Brunei, China, Indonesia, Malaysia, Thailand
South Asian Nations	Bangladesh, Bhutan, India, Nepal, Pakistan, Sikkim, Sri Lanka
Southeast Asian Nations	Brunei, Burma (Myanmar), Indonesia, Cambodia (Kampuchea), Laos, Malaysia, Philippines, Singapore, Thailand, Vietnam

GLOSSARY

■ General

Bureaucratic Capitalists: A specific term for a phenomenon primarily associated with the Republican Era in China (usually 1928-1945). The term reflects both the traditional importance of the civil servant in society and also the newly recognized power associated with the accumulation of wealth through capital investment. Bureaucratic capitalism represented the pinnacle of power in Republican China, where four wealthy extended families maintained dominance in both politics and economics and utilized that dominance to influence the domestic and international policies of their nation in both spheres.

City-state: Usually refers to a small self-governing region. Singapore is an excellent example, as it is simply a large city which is an independent nation. Sometimes the term is applied to Hong Kong, although technically this is incorrect, as Hong Kong is a British Crown Colony until mid-1997.

Education Mama: A term applied to (often zealous) Japanese mothers who drive their children to high academic achievement. Mothers usually play a large role in their children's education, by identifying the best school and ensuring that their children study hard.

In the Japanese educational system, all schools are ranked relative to one another. Entry to one of the top universities virtually guarantees a job at a prestigious firm after graduation. This means that children must go to the "best" high school, to increase their chances of entry to a top university. In order to get into the "best" high school, one must attend the "best" junior high. The situation is so extreme that there is stiff competition for entry to the "best" nursery schools!

GDP: Acronym for Gross Domestic Product. Refers to revenue from production *only*, and not to revenue from services or from extra-national sources. The GDP is smaller than the GNP.

Import Substitution: The promotion of domestic manufacture through special import tariffs, or through subsidies to domestic industries, or a combination of the two. This encourages the growth of developing industry by protecting it from foreign competition.

International Monetary Fund (IMF): Affiliated with the UN, the IMF provides international credit, in order to develop stable exchange rates and world-wide fiscal cooperation.

Meritocracy: A term that has been coined to indicate bureaucratic advancement based on ability (rather than birth). Meritocracies are characterized by civil service and advancement based on an individual's achievements. Ideally, a meritocracy is open to all, regardless of gender, race, religion, status, wealth, birth, etc.

NIE: Acronym for Newly Industrialized Economy. These states have industrialized only within this century, hence the name. Commonly (but not exclusively) applied to Hong Kong, Singapore, South Korea, and Taiwan. These four are also known as "the Little Dragons" or "the Little Tigers" for their tenacity in the world marketplace and their ambitious (and successful) rise. NIC, standing for Newly Industrialized Country, is a synonymous term.

Osaka: A major city in Western Japan, Osaka is Japan's third largest city, with only Tokyo and Yokohama exceeding it. Osaka and the Osaka-Kobe belt are centers for finance and industry, second only to the Tokyo-Yokohama zone.

Some of the oldest archaeological sites in Japan are in the Osaka region. The site of many temples and long a center for trade with China, it was also Toyotomi Hideyoshi's base of operations and site of his castle. Although it burned down in 1868, a new Osaka castle was built in 1931 and serves as a park and museum. During Tokugawa times, literature and theater flourished in the Osaka area. In addition to its financial importance, modern Osaka has numerous universities, libraries, and museums.

Scholar-Bureaucrat: In the traditional Chinese Confucian hierarchy, the top grouping of the four classes of commoners were those who were both Confucian scholars and civil servants. The traditional Chinese examination system required all civil servants be Confucian scholars; however, not all scholars were in government service. In order to be considered a member of the most prestigious class, a man had to be both classically trained and officially appointed by the central government.

Taiwan: An island off the southern coast of China, Taiwan's official name is the Republic of China. Although a part of China, it has been ruled by foreign powers for much of its modern history. The Portuguese named it Formosa ("beautiful"); later, the Dutch took control. Japan was the first to develop Taiwan, which was acquired as spoils of the 1894-95 Sino-Japanese War. After Japan's defeat in WWII, Taiwan reverted again to Chinese control.

After the KMT lost the 1945-49 Chinese Civil War, they fled to Taiwan. The roughly two million Mandarin-speaking refugees imposed themselves as rulers on top of the approximately nine million Min-speaking native Taiwanese. (There are also about 200,000 aborigines.) The KMT, headed by Chiang Kai-shek, continued its authoritarian rule in Taiwan. After Chiang's death in 1975, native Taiwanese finally gained access to government. In 1988, Lee Teng-hui, a native Taiwanese, became president of the republic.

Taiwan has flourished economically, partly due to generous US support, but mostly due to intense industrialization and a focus on education. Still, agriculture remains a significant part of the economy.

■ South Korea

Chaebol: (cha bowl) Large industrial-commercial combines with interests in many fields. The four largest are Hanjin, Hyundai, Lucky, and Samsung. Another significant *chaebol* is Daewoo. *Chaebol* are the Korean equivalent of Japan's *keiretsu,* or the prewar *zaibatsu.*

EPB: Acronym for Economic Planning Board. Formed in 1961, the EPB plans and directs Korean economic development at the governmental level. The head of the EPB is always the current Deputy Prime Minister. Primarily composed of economists and technocrats, the EPB has directed Korean industry from an import substitution policy to an export-led economy. In some regards, the EPB is similar to Japan's MITI.

Han: (hahn) Korean term for Korea and Korean identity. Although homophonic with the Chinese Han, these two terms are written with different characters.

Han Minjok: A Korean term which literally means "Korean people," and has come to mean "Korean nation" as well.

Hyundai: (hewn dye) One of the four largest *chaebol*, Hyundai is best known in America for its automobiles. In Korea, it is the largest shipbuilding company. It also has interests in furniture and computers. 10% of Hyundai is owned by Mitsubishi, one of the modern Japanese *keiretsu*.

KAL: Acronym for Korean Air Lines.

Park Chung Hee: (pahk choong he) 1917-1979. Park entered the Japanese military academy in 1940, graduated in 1944, and served for one year as a second lieutenant in the Japanese army. After WWII, he entered the South Korean Constabulary.

In 1947, Park was recruited by communists and participated in an anti-government conspiracy. He was discovered and sentenced to death. However, he saved his life by turning informant; the information he gave led to the deaths of many communist operatives. Reinstated in the army after the Korean War broke out, he performed well and rose to the rank of major-general.

Even before Syngman Rhee was deposed, Park and other dissidents had been planning a coup. They acted on 16 May 1961, ousting the unprepared civilian government of Chang Myon. Park became acting president in 1962 and president in 1963. He remained president until his assassination in 1979.

Although Korea prospered economically under Park, his politics went from oppressive to regressive as he flouted the constitution and eventually replaced it with his own authoritarian version. He had become increasingly autocratic and withdrawn when he was assassinated by his own Korean CIA director on 26 October 1979. Park was succeeded by Prime Minister Choi Kyu Ha.

Syngman Rhee: 1875-1965. Syngman Rhee was first educated in missionary schools in Korea. Later, he studied at George Washington,

Harvard, and Princeton universities. He fought tirelessly for the Korean cause both at home and abroad.

Rhee's efforts for his country began at the end of the nineteenth century; he was jailed in 1897 for his involvement with the reformist Independence Club. While in jail he converted to Christianity. He worked for Korean independence during Japanese rule, first in Korea as a YMCA teacher and missionary, then, from 1913 to 1940, in Hawaii. In 1919, Rhee was selected president of the Shanghai-based Korean Provisional Government-in-Exile. Due to his poor relations with the Provisional Government, Rhee was impeached in 1925, but he refused to recognize this action.

During WWII, he was in Washington DC, where he won many admirers for his staunch anti-Soviet and anti-communist stances. He returned to Korea in 1945, and was elected the first president of the Republic of Korea in 1948. Re-elected in 1952, 1956, and 1960, he never gave up his desire to "march north" and forcibly unify the country. Although widely respected by the Korean people, he was unable to work with others, and had little understanding of economics. These two factors retarded Korea's postwar growth, and were cause for growing opposition to him and his rule. His supporters became increasingly dependant on fraud and coercion to keep him in power. All this, along with blatant election fraud in the 1960 elections, popular demonstrations, and police brutality, led to his resignation. He died in exile in Honolulu in 1965.

ROK: Abbreviation for Republic of Korea, which is South Korea.

ROK-Japan Normalization Treaty: Signed on 22 June 1965. Earlier attempts at normalization had failed for many reasons, including Korea's demands for enormous reparations and Syngman Rhee's uncompromising nature.

The treaty covered a broad range of issues. Central to the Koreans was formal nullification of all agreements and treaties between Japan and Korea which were signed on or before 22 April 1910--the date of Korea's annexation by Japan. The treaty also recognized the ROK as the sole legitimate government on the peninsula. Japan agreed to give permanent resident status to all Koreans living in Japan since prior to WWII. Japan agreed to pay only a fraction of the reparations demanded earlier, and the treaty gave Japanese fishermen access to Korean waters. These provisions were denounced by the opposition parties and were cause for student demonstrations. However, the treaty also stipulated that Japan would provide capital and loans, as well as open up opportunities for trade and investments.

The depth of mistrust between Japan and Korea is illustrated by the fact that it was not until twenty years after the Japanese colonial government left Korea that a treaty was signed. Although relations are better now than they were earlier in this century, there is still a powerful undercurrent of tension across the Korea Strait.

Second Republic: 19 August 1960 to 18 May 1961 are the dates for the short-lived Second Republic under Chang Myon. After the fall of Syngman Rhee, elections were held and Chang Myon was elected as prime minister to Korea's first democratic government. After a period of initial uncertainty, the Chang cabinet was beginning to achieve and progress when, on 16 May 1961, General Park Chung Hee lead a successful military coup against the democratically-elected civilian government. This was the end of the Second Republic and the start of the Third Republic of Park Chung Hee.

Seoul: First selected as the capital of the Yi in 1394, Seoul is today the capital of the Republic of (South) Korea. With mountains in the north, Seoul's growth has spread both to the south, across the Han River, and to the east. West from Seoul lie both Inchon and the Yellow Sea.

Although Seoul expanded during the Japanese occupation, the city was virtually demolished during the Korean War. Since the end of the war, Seoul has grown rapidly, with elevated highways, tunnels, and subways built to handle the increasing traffic congestion.

Seoul is central to all aspects of modern South Korea. It has a plethora of churches, company headquarters, hospitals, hotels, museums, and universities. Its selection as the site for the 1988 Summer Olympics was widely viewed as a crowning achievement in the city's (and the country's) postwar rebirth and growth.

USAMGIK: Acronym for United States Army Military Government in Korea.

Won: (won) The Korean unit of currency.

■ Southeast Asia

ASEAN: Acronym for Association of Southeast Asian Nations. Formed on 8 August 1967; member states are Brunei (joined 1984), Indonesia, Malaysia, the Philippines, Singapore, and Thailand. In contrast to NATO, the Warsaw Pact, and SEATO, all of which were formed for mutual defense purposes, the stated goal of ASEAN is promotion of economic development and cooperation. ASEAN, however, has been more significant as a political than an economic organization, particularly in regard to relations with Vietnam and Cambodia.

ASEAN-4: Indonesia, Malaysia, the Philippines, and Thailand. They are defined by their general size and low- to middle-income developing economies.

Brunei: An oil-exporting sultanate on the island of Borneo, Brunei gained its independence from Great Britain on 1 January 1984. It joined ASEAN that very month.

Brunei faces the South China Sea. Malay is the primary language; English and Chinese are also spoken. Islam is the official religion. The population of Brunei is 65% Malay and 20% Chinese.

Although it also has rubber and timber, Brunei's primary exports are petroleum and natural gas, giving the country one of the world's highest per capita incomes. A wide range of social services are provided without charge to Brunei's citizens. The Sultan of Brunei is both its leader and the richest man in the world.

Burma: Burma (the current government has adopted the name Myanmar) is a federation of five states and shares borders with Bangladesh, China, India, Laos, and Thailand. Burma's coastline is on the Bay of Bengal and the Andanam Sea. About 75% of the population is Burmese, and there are several ethnic minorities, including Chinese, Indian, Karen, and Shan. Burmese is the official language; Buddhism is the dominant faith. Rangoon is the capital and largest city. Approximately 80% of the population live in rural areas.

Agriculture is Burma's economic forte. Rice is the main crop; it is also the world leader in teak production. Although the country has abundant mineral deposits, these resources are grossly underutilized. This is attributed to the inefficient socialist military government which has ruled Burma since 2 March 1962. Under this regime, Burma has declined into poverty and political unrest. In spite of Burma's potential wealth, Burma applied for "Least-Developed Nation" status in 1986, in order to increase the amount of aid it could receive.

Lee Kuan Yew: (lee kwahn you) Born 1923. Prime Minister of Singapore from 1959 to 1990; popularly known as "Uncle Harry." His rule was often likened to that of a traditional Confucian bureaucrat, as he shaped policies in accordance with his paternalistic view of what was best for the state. One of his better-known statements is, "we decide what is right; never mind what the people think." Regardless, Singapore's economy flourished under Lee.

QUESTIONS FOR REVIEW

1. Look at the list of Key Concepts and Names for this chapter. Find all the place names, then locate each place on the maps in the text.

2. Describe the pattern of policy choices made by the each Asian capitalist economy.

3. What are the key elements of the Asian model of economic development? What factors are the same as those in the West? What factors are different?

4. What is import substitution? How has it been used in Pacific Asia?

5. What is the importance of ASEAN? What kind of an organization is it? What binds the countries together? What economic factors separate them in spite of their unity in ASEAN?

6. How are the "ASEAN-4" different from the other ASEAN states? How is Indonesia different from other ASEAN states?

7. Which countries are classified as NIEs? What characterizes their development? What are their differences? their similarities?

8. Why are the NIEs in a different economic category from Japan? Compare and contrast the NIEs and Japan.

9. How, and to what extent, do the NIEs, ASEAN, and Japan depend on the global economy?

10. What is the significance of the US to the South Korean economy? How did international developments affect the ROK?

11. What is the relationship between natural resources and primary product economies? Compare resource-rich areas with Hong Kong and Singapore. What accounts for the difference in growth between Hong Kong and Singapore versus countries rich in natural resources?

ADDITIONAL RECOMMENDED READINGS

Amsden, Alice H. *Asia's Next Giant: South Korea and Late Industrialization.* New York: Oxford University Press, 1989.

Berger, Peter L. and Hsiao Hsing-huang, eds. *In Search of an East Asian Development Model.* New Brunswick: Transaction Publishers, 1988.

Eckert, Carter J., et. al. *Korea Old and New: A History.* Seoul: Ilchokak Publishers, 1990.

106

Haggard, Stephen. *Pathways from the Periphery: The Politics of Growth in the Newly Industrialized Countries.* Ithaca, NY: Cornell University Press, 1990.

Tai, Hung-chao, ed. *Confucianism and Economic Development: An Oriental Alternative?* Washington, DC: Washington Institute Press, 1989.

UNIT NINE

Power, Authority, and the Advent of Democracy

OVERVIEW

The spectacular economic growth in the Asia Pacific region has also given rise to certain tensions and conflicts within each society, particularly between dictatorial governments (which often legitimate themselves by the need for economic control) and the populist assertions of their citizens. It is a tension that transcends economic ideology, having arisen in both communist China and capitalist South Korea. This unit examines that tension in countries where a new generation of political leaders has begun to interact with the aspirations of a more prosperous and self-confident middle class.

Traditional attitudes toward power and authority have a lasting influence, regardless of the pace of social and economic change. Even where a democratic government is strong, as in Japan, it operates in a far different manner than in Europe or the United States--and, in some ways, in a more effective manner. Democracy is not an Anglo-Saxon patent. Where democracy fights to be established, it must do battle on different grounds, among peoples who may value harmony as highly as justice. The West cannot expect Asia-Pacific nations to set such great import on individualism or the adversary method of legal proceedings.

The example of South Korea is instructive since it faces the choice between authoritarian government and democracy more clearly than most nations, partly as a result of its great economic successes. With the end of the Japanese occupation, which lasted for nearly half a century, Korea was suddenly thrown onto its own resources. Once a ruthless Stalinist system appeared in North Korea, the South was less likely to rely on anything but a powerful central authority. This was first personified by the elderly and dogmatic Syngman Rhee, who represented the traditional Korean preference for referring virtually all decisions to an authoritarian father figure. President Park Chung Hee played a similar role until his assassination. During his 18-year rule, he presided over Korea's industrialization. A crisis grew in Korea's government under President Chung Doo Hwan until popular pressures even within the ruling Democratic Justice Party forced a wide-open Presidential election that became a pivotal event in modern

Korean history. The tensions between past authoritarian approaches to governance in Korea, rationalized in part by calls for a disciplined, Confucian society, and the desire for a more open, democratic system, continue.

In Thailand, communist insurgencies were largely suppressed and there was no colonial legacy. Yet the Thais find themselves "drifting towards democracy" in the wake of successive military coups. In Indonesia, the role of the military in maintaining stability continues to be paramount. The gestures toward democracy seem often like the posturings of the traditional *wayang kulit* shadow puppet plays. Malaysia walks a tightrope of ethnic division. Underneath its high-rise modernity, the city-state of Singapore has its own brand of tension between democracy and authoritarianism.

The factors that support or oppose democratic rule vary widely throughout the Asia Pacific region. They include the experience of colonial rule, the perceptions of internal and external threats, the dimensions of traditional political authority, the lofty apolitical role of a monarchy (in Thailand), shifting patron-client relationships (Philippines), and the stress on an "infallible" central Confucian authority in Korea.

STUDY RESOURCES

Video: "The Fight for Democracy"
Text: Chapter 8: *Power, Authority, and the Advent of Democracy*

STUDY FOCUS

After viewing the video and reading Chapter 8, you should have a basic understanding of the following concepts.

1.   Asian efforts to achieve working democratic governments have resulted in systems which are adapted to Asian, rather than Anglo-American, perceptions of how democracy can function in their societies.

2.   Post–WWII developments have been an experimental process of transition to erect Western democratic forms within traditional frameworks of power and authority.

3.   In Asia societies, the maintenance of stability and order have often taken priority over democratic processes of power-sharing.

4. Democratization in South Korea has been complicated by the North-South division of the peninsula, but political liberalization has allowed a more open discussion of societal problems.

5. In Taiwan, Thailand, Malaysia, Indonesia, the Philippines, and Korea, democracy has begun to be exercised in varying degrees and forms.

KEY CONCEPTS AND NAMES

This is a list of important terms, people, and places that you should understand from reading the text. If you cannot think of a brief explanation for everything on this list, you need to read the text again.

Alliance Party	KMT
Benigno Aquino	Kwangju Massacre
Corazon Aquino	Lee Teng-hui
Authoritarianism	Mahathir Mohamad
King Bhumibol (Rama IX)	Malay
Bumiputera	Ferdinand Marcos
Chiang Ching-kuo	*Musyawarah*
Chun Doo Hwan	Nationalism
Communal Politics	New Korea Democratic Party
Confucianism	*Pancasila*
Crony Capit	People's Party
Democratic Justice Party (DJP)	PKI
Democratic Liberal Party (DLP)	Roh Tae Woo
Democratic Progressive Party	Suharto
GOLKAR	Sukarno
Guided Democracy	UMNO

GLOSSARY

■ Indonesia

Abangan: (uh bun gun) Indonesian form of religion which combines elements of animism, Buddhism, Hinduism, and Islam.

GOLKAR: From *golongan karya,* "functional group," a part of Sukarno's Guided Democracy which has been retained by Suharto. Representing Indonesian political value as "functional" rather than competitive, GOLKAR emphasizes social mobilization for projects with broad national import by channeling mass energies.

The concept, originally introduced during Sukarno's tenure, proclaimed the unity of all Indonesians, regardless of their location in the archipelago. While promoting nationalism, on the one hand, it also has as its intended effect the legitimization of military rule; both Sukarno and Suharto have manipulated the concept for this purpose. Initially, GOLKAR established the authority of the military and civil bureaucracy over all other groups and was thereby used to quash the growing popularity of the Indonesian Communist Party in the mid-1960s. In 1969, Golkor was declared a political party and it has exerted considerable control over government and politics since the early 1970s.

Guided Democracy: The political form developed by Sukarno in 1959 to resolve the basic conflicts in national politics (e.g., role of religions, military/civilian divisiveness, tensions between Java and the outer islands) through utilizing the Javanese concept of *musyawarah*. Indonesian presidential power shifted from dealing directly with these problems to developing consensus and guiding national policy.

Mufakat: (moo fuh cut) "Consensus." A part of the political process in Indonesia derived from traditional Javanese thought.

Musyawarah: (moose yuh wuh ruh) "Deliberation." A political process also derived from traditional Javanese thought.

Abdul Haris Nasution: (uhb dool huh reese nuh soo tea own) Born 1918. Nasution received military training from the Dutch. After WWII, he rose to the rank of general and held various commands. Nasution's support of Sukarno was instrumental in establishing Guided Democracy. Though a critic of Suharto, Nasution was active in post-1965 politics. In 1966, he was elected chairman of Parliament, a post he held until 1972.

New Order: Suharto's government, the main features of which are *Pancasila*, political stability, economic growth, and a restrained international profile.

Pancasila: (pun kuh see luh) The "five pillars" of state ideology developed by Sukarno. Consists of: 1, belief in One God; 2, nationalism; 3, international cooperation; 4, democracy; and 5, social justice.

Suharto: Born 1921. Took power from Sukarno in 1966 after the unsuccessful PKI coup. Suharto led the drive to eliminate the PKI after the coup. He copied many of Sukarno's tactics, but applied them in a rightist manner, as opposed to Sukarno's leftist inclination.

Wayang kulit: (wuh yuhng koo lit) The traditional shadow puppet theater of Indonesia. Flat puppets, hand operated with sticks, are placed on the inside of a backlit screen. Just the shadows of the puppets are seen by the audience. The stories are performed in classical language, deal with traditional themes, and usually have a moral.

■ Malaysia

Alliance Party: Led by UMNO, this united front was created to satisfy British demands in the 1950s and was a necessary step in the process of gaining independence from Britain.

BN: *"Barison Nacional,"* the National Front. Developed from the reorganization of the Alliance Party in 1971.

Bumiputera: (boo me poo truh) Literally "sons of the soil," this is the official term for Malays and the indigenous peoples of the outer Malaysian areas, Sabah and Sarawak, on the island of Borneo.

Communal Politics: A term reflective of the Malaysian plural society, which developed from 1800 on, as each major ethnic group tended to settle in separate areas--Malays in the villages, Chinese in the towns, and Indians on the plantations. Each community is a tight-knit ethnic structure, grouped by language, religion, and educational system. Each community has developed separate political organizations to reflect their ethnicity; this has resulted in ethnic factionalism.

MCA: The Malayan Chinese Association, a political party whose members are ethnic Chinese.

MIC: The Malayan Indian Congress, an ethnic political party consisting of Indians.

Datuk Seri Mahathir Mohamad: (duh too-k sree muh huh tier) Born 1925. The fourth Prime Minister of Malaysia and concurrently head of UMNO, Dr. Mahathir succeeded to the office from the position of Deputy Prime Minister in 1981. Coming from a commoner background with no apparent ties to any of the Malay royal house and training as a medical doctor rather than a lawyer, Dr. Mahathir broke the precedents set by the first three Malaysian PMs. Although a *bumiputera* and an advocate of Malay rights, Dr. Mahathir spoke out strongly against UMNO leadership after the 1969 riots and was temporarily ousted from the party. His leadership has resulted in increasing government efficiency, eliminating corruption in the public sector, but his confrontational political style has caused schisms within his party and has resulted in fewer political freedoms. In the economic sphere, Dr. Mahathir has stressed development of heavy industries based on Malaysian energy and raw material resources and has attempted to invigorate the *bumiputera* work ethic with the challenging examples of Japan and South Korea. In foreign relations, Mahathir's "Look East" policy has resulted in closer cooperation with regional partners Japan and South Korea at the expense of ties with Great Britain.

Tunku Abdul Rahman Alhaj: (tune coo uhb dool ruh muhn ul huhj) Born 1903. Son of a sultan (*tunku* means "prince"), Rahman led the Malayan independence movement and served as first prime minister (1957-1970). Honored as *Bapa Malaysia*--"Father of Malaysia."

13 May Rioting: An eruption of communal rioting in reaction to the apparent loss of ethnic Malay primacy in the 1969 elections, these bloody ethnic clashes resulted in a high death toll (several hundreds of Chinese). By 1971, the issue had been resolved by guaranteeing Malay political dominance and preservation of Malay cultural heritage.

UMNO: The United Malays National Organization. The dominant political party of Malaysia, consisting of ethnic Malays, who constitute an ethnic majority and an economic minority in Malaysia. Malaysia's four prime ministers have all come from UMNO.

■ Philippines

Benigno Aquino: 1932-1983. Born to a renowned political family, he was the "wonder boy" of Philippine politics. A war journalist at seventeen, governor at twenty-nine, senator at thirty-three, Benigno was the leading candidate for president in the 1973 Filipino election, which was cancelled by Marcos' imposition of martial law. Aquino was arrested by Marcos in 1972, tried, and sentenced to death by a Marcos military court in 1977. However, he was released in 1980, to go to the US for heart surgery. Upon returning to his homeland in August 1983, he was immediately assassinated by Marcos' security forces.

Corazon Aquino: Born 1933. Born in the provinces, "Cory" moved with her family to the US, where she completed high school and college. In 1954 she married Benigno Aquino in Manila and became a homemaker. After her husband's arrest in 1972, she became his liaison to those who opposed Marcos. After Benigno's assassination, Cory became the symbol of his democratic reform policies and the opposition candidate to Marcos in the 1985 elections. Buoyed by enthusiastic popular support and the "people power" revolution, Corazon Aquino claimed victory in the contested election of February 1986 and became the seventh president of the Philippines. Initially, Cory Aquino, who represented no defined political party, enjoyed widespread popular support. That support declined amid several attempted coups by dissident military factions and worsening Filipino economic conditions.

Ferdinand Marcos: 1917-1990. A member of the Philippine establishment elite, Marcos served as Philippine president from his election in 1965, and as virtual dictator after his 1972 imposition of martial law, until his forced relocation to Hawaii in 1986. Marcos and his powerful wife, Imelda, became increasingly supportive of repressive and corrupt practices by their regime, propped up by massive US aid, amid worsening political and economic conditions in the country. His miscalculation of the strength of the opposition "people power" movement led to his hasty evacuation by the US to Hawaii.

People Power: Reference to the 1980s development of a grassroots movement among "commoners" against the increasing political repression and economic oppression of Marcos and the "Crony Capitalists." This combination of groups united in a call for honesty in the 1986 election, which was Marcos' first major political defeat.

Peso: The unit of Philippine currency.

■ **Singapore**

Political Action Party (PAP): The ruling party of Singapore.

■ **South Korea**

Chuch'e: (chew cheh) "Self-reliance." The official political philosophy of North Korea, it is a mix of independence and Marxism-Leninism blended to suit North Korea.

Chun Doo Hwan: (chun doo hwahn) Born in 1931. Chun was elected president of the Fifth Republic of Korea in 1981. His achievements include lifting martial law, reducing inflation, promoting a new constitution which included a limit on presidents to a single seven-year term, and turning a negative-growth economy around. On the negative side, he suppressed independent publishers and sent more than 30,000 people to jail on political charges. Roo Tae Woo succeeded Chun as president in the elections of 1987.

Democratic Liberal Party (DLP): The ruling party of South Korea, which represents big business, the bureaucracy, the military, and some left-wing elements. The DLP is modeled after Japan's LDP.

Kim Dae Jung: (kim deh joong) A prominent opposition politician, he has been imprisoned several times, and in 1980 escaped death at the hands of the South Korean government due only to international pressure (primarily the US). He ran for president in 1969, stunning the repressive Park regime by winning 43.6% of the vote, and ran a close third in the 1987 presidential elections.

Kim Young Sam: Born 1927. Educated at Seoul National University. During martial law, he was banned from politics. A prominent opposition politician who finished second in the 1987 elections, Kim joined the coalition party formed by President Roh Tae Woo in 1990.

Kwangju Incident: (kwahng jew) Also known as the Kwangju Massacre. After the assassination of President Park Chung Hee on 26 October 1979, there were enormous student-led demonstrations in the eastern coastal city of Kwangju. The army moved in to suppress the demonstrations, and more than 200 students were killed.

The Kwangju Incident continues to serve as a rallying point in Korean politics, particularly for the opposition led by Kim Dae Jung.

New Korea Democratic Party: Formed in 1985, this party is a combination of smaller opposition parties.

Roh Tae Woo: (no teh woo) Born 1932. A former general, Roh, representing the DLP, was elected president in 1987.

■ Taiwan

Chiang Ching-kuo: (jahng jing gwoe) 1910-1988. Eldest son of Chiang Kai-shek; educated in the Soviet Union. Chiang Ching-kuo held various posts in the KMT government in China. After the Nationalist retreat to Taiwan in 1949, he was groomed to be his father's successor. He became vice-premier in 1969, premier in 1972, and president in 1978, a post he held until his death. Although unwaveringly dedicated to the Nationalist cause, he was also concerned with the lot of common people. During his rule, the number of Taiwanese (i.e., those not born on the mainland) participating in politics increased markedly.

Democratic Progressive Party: The main opposition party of Taiwanese politics.

Lee Teng-hui: (lee dung hway) Born 1923. Became the third president of Taiwan after Chiang Ching-guo's death in office in 1988. Lee is the first native Taiwanese to become president of Taiwan. Political liberalization continues under Lee.

■ Thailand

Bhumibol Adulyadej (Rama IX): Born in 1927 in Cambridge, Massachusetts; grandson of Chulalongkorn. Crowned in 1950, King Bhumibol has been a source of political stability amid the passage of many civilian and military Thai governments. His reign has increased the prestige of the monarchy to a degree that has made him the most respected and revered figure in Thailand.

TIME-FRAME QUESTIONS

1. a. Bloodless Thai coup which instituted constitutional government.
   b. Election of Chatichai Choonhavan to premiership.
   c. Thai coup led by Sunthorn Kongsompong.
   d. First postwar Thai coup.
   e. Bhumibol ascends to the Thai throne.

2. a. 13 May rioting.
   b. Mahathir Mohamad becomes prime minister.
   c. Tuku Abdul Rahman declares Malaysia's independence.
   d. Formation of *Barison Nacional*.
   e. Musa Hitam resigns.

3. a. Indonesia declared independent.
   b. Suharto elected president.
   c. Parliamentary rule abandoned in Indonesia.
   d. Fall of Sukarno.
   e. West New Guinea incorporated into Indonesia.

4. a. Cory Aquino elected president of Philippines.
   b. Benigno Aquino assassinated.
   c. Marcos proclaims martial law.
   d. Marcos dies in exile.
   e. Marcos elected president.

5. a. Roh Tae Woo elected president of South Korea.
   b. Syngman Rhee declares martial law.
   c. Chang Myon elected president.
   d. Chun Doo Hwan elected president.
   e. Park Chun Hee assassinated.

116

6. a. Taiwan declares end of "communist rebellion."
    b. Death of Chiang Ching-kuo.
    c. Formation of DPP.
    d. Sino-British Joint Declaration on Hong Kong.
    e. Lee Teng-hui becomes president.

QUESTIONS FOR REVIEW

1. Re-read the final section of Chapter 8. How does democracy vary from country to country in Pacific Asia? Compare and contrast each country's experience with democratic forms.

2. What traditional elements of governance were incorporated into the modern Indonesian state? How has that affected "democracy?"

3. What is "Limited Democracy?" What does it mean to Malaysia? Why was it incorporated into Malaysian politics?

4. Who was Ferdinand Marcos? How did he rule?

5. Where and how has colonialism affected politics in Pacific Asia?

6. What is meant by "Guided Democracy?"

7. What political role has the military played in Thailand? in Indonesia? in South Korea? Compare and contrast.

ADDITIONAL RECOMMENDED READINGS

Bresnan, John, ed. *Crisis in the Philippines: The Marcos Era and Beyond.* Princeton, NJ: Princeton University Press, 1986.

Esposito, John L. *Islam in Asia: Religion, Politics, and Society.* New York: Oxford University Press, 1987.

Kim, Joungwon Alexander. *Divided Korea: The Politics of Development 1945-1972.* Cambridge, MA: East Asian Research Center, Harvard University, 1975.

von Vorys, Karl. *Democracy Without Consensus: Communalism and Political Stability in Malaysia.* Princeton, NJ: Princeton University Press, 1976.

Wurfel, David and Bruce Burton. *The Political Economy of Foreign Policy in Southeast Asia.* New York: St. Martin's Press, 1990.

UNIT TEN

Sentimental Imperialists: America in Asia

OVERVIEW

The end of the nineteenth century marked the debut of the United States as a colonial power in the Pacific. The annexation of the Philippines and the Hawaiian Islands followed victory in the Spanish-American War. American expansionism differed from traditional European colonialism, thanks to the pluralistic tradition of the United States. Americans felt that Asians should become "Americanized," not merely the subjects of a colonial power. Along with the intense proselytizing efforts of American Christian missions in East Asia there was a strain of racial superiority. This found an outlet in the exclusion laws directed against Chinese and Japanese in the 1920s, as well as overbearing paternalism in the Philippines and various examples of anti-Asian "whites only" prejudice. Old-fashioned chauvinism was also involved, as Americans began to have proprietary feelings toward the Pacific as an "American" ocean.

There are comparisons and contrasts to be drawn with other nations in the region, notably the Philippines. As a result of a long-standing American commitment, the Philippines finally achieved post-colonial independence after World War II. Yet over the years, Philippine politics--barring the 1950s interregnum of the charismatic President Ramon Magsaysay--devolved into a two-party system divided by personalities and controlled by dictatorial local power brokers. In effect, this represented a return to the centuries-old system of domination by the small ruling elite, with minorities and the rural poor given no effective voice in national policy-making.

The culmination of this system was the dictatorship of Ferdinand Marcos, who turned his country into a virtual private kingdom. The video segment uses the example of the Philippines to show both the ill-advised US support of Marcos--almost to the end of his rule--and the unsurprising growth of armed communist guerilla resistance to the Philippine government.

American policy toward China is another focus of the video segment, for it was in China more than the Philippines that the tragedy of the American postwar strategy in Asia was born. The search

118

for culprits upon whom to blame the "loss" of China to the communists reverberated in American politics for two decades and decimated the ranks of capable Asia expertise in the government.

The postwar policy of "containment" was militarized in the course of the Korean War, a civil war in which Americans participated but which they only vaguely understood. In its aftermath, shaped by the "Red scare" in domestic politics, there emerged an inflexible US strategy to "pay any price" to stop communism throughout the world. The war in Vietnam became the ultimate price of that strategy, and only with the decision to conclude the war and change the policies that underlay containment in ways that emphasized a global and regional balance of power did the United States manage to successfully integrate Pacific Asia into its global contest with the Soviet Union.

STUDY RESOURCES

Video: "Sentimental Imperialists"
Text: Chapter 9: *Sentimental Imperialists: America in Asia*

STUDY FOCUS

After viewing the video and reading Chapter 9, you should have a basic understanding of the following concepts:

1.   America encountered self-contradictions when it entered the twentieth century as an advocate of democracy and freedom, yet was also an imperial power in the Philippines.

2.   A misperception of China, its leaders, and Sino-American relations left Americans believing that they had "lost" China to conspiratorial communism, thus exaggerating their fear of communism in Asia.

3.   Americans underestimated nationalist aspirations in Asia as the basis for independence movements.

4.   Domestic politics have influenced US foreign policy in Asia, and vice-versa.

5.   Containment policies changed over time, profoundly affecting how the US met the challenge of communism during the Cold War.

KEY CONCEPTS AND NAMES

This is a list of important terms, people, and places that you should understand from reading the text. If you cannot think of a brief explanation for everything on this list, you need to read the text again.

ASEAN
CCP
Domino Theory
DPRK
Kim Il Sung
Henry Kissinger
KMT
Korean War
KPR
Mao Zedong
Pat McCarran
Joseph McCarthy
Ngo Dinh Diem

Nguyen Van Thieu
Richard Nixon
Nixon Doctrine
NSC-68
Policy of Containment
Syngman Rhee
ROK
Tet Offensive
Harry S. Truman
Truman Doctrine
UN
Viet Cong

GLOSSARY

■ General

Henry Kissinger: Born in 1923 in Germany; became a naturalized US citizen. Dr. Kissinger was well recognized as a scholar before he served as special assistant for National Security and Secretary of State under Presidents Nixon and Ford. Kissinger is considered the architect of the Nixon Doctrine. In 1971, Kissinger secretly travelled to China, meeting with Zhou Enlai in Beijing to arrange Nixon's unprecedented trip to the PRC. Considered one of America's "elder statesmen," he was recognized by the international community in 1975, when he shared the Nobel Peace Prize with the Foreign Minister of North Vietnam, Le Duc Tho.

MACV: Acronym for Military Assistance Command Vietnam.

Pat McCarran: 1876-1954. Conservative Democrat from Nevada. Elected to the US Senate in 1933; served until his death in 1954. McCarran sponsored legislation designed to track down "hidden" communists in the US by making them register and used his committee to interrogate American public officials about their political affiliations.

Joseph R. McCarthy: 1908-1957. A WWII veteran, Joseph McCarthy tapped the feelings of fear in postwar America to build a political base in 1946, when he was elected to the US Senate from Wisconsin as a Republican. Flamboyant and ever ready to capitalize on events, Senator McCarthy dominated the political scene that took its character and name from him--"McCarthyism." The Senator made a sensation by publicly declaring that he had the names of some fifty individuals in the US government who were known to have been members of the American Communist Party ("card-carrying") or were known to have been friends with Communists or to have associated with known Communists. McCarthyism became characterized by these sensational allegations, which were never proved or substantiated in the least degree. However, countless government careers, public reputations, and even private lives were ruined by the Senator's charges. When McCarthy began to investigate the US Army, the fraud became vividly apparent. This resulted in his formal censure by the US Senate in 1954. He died in office in 1957.

Richard Nixon: Prominent conservative Republican politician. He served as a Representative from California (1946-52); Eisenhower's vice president (1952-60); and US president (1968-73). He is the only American president to resign from office. While a Congressman, Nixon was a prominent member of HUAC (the House Un-American Activities Committee), which, as the House equivalent of the McCarran Committee, sought to rid American society of "subversive Communist" influences.

Nixon Doctrine: (also called the "Guam Doctrine") Enunciated by President Richard Nixon on the Pacific island of Guam in July 1969, the Nixon Doctrine consisted of three propositions:

"First, the United States will keep all of its treaty commitments.

Second, we shall provide a shield if a nuclear power threatens the freedom of a nation allied with us or of a nation whose survival we consider vital to our security.

Third, in cases involving other types of aggression, we shall furnish military and economic assistance when requested in accordance with our treaty commitments. But we shall look to the nation directly threatened to assume the primary responsibility of providing the manpower for its defense."

The final sentence signaled that the United States would expect far more of its allies in Asia and elsewhere to assume the burden of defense against communism, and that South Vietnam, in particular, would be required to assume a greater manpower burden as the United States withdrew its troops.

Policy of Containment: As enunciated by George Kennan in the late 1940s, the United States policy of containment sought initially to block Soviet expansionism in the world by a variety of political, economic, and military means. Victory in World War II had positioned the Red Army so that it was capable of attacking and possibly taking control of the two great power centers of the War, Germany and Japan. Soviet antipathy toward the West, and its influence over communist parties worldwide, presented an additional threat. If contained long enough, Kennan argued, the worldwide communist network would break up due to the chronic Soviet inability to tolerate diversity. He predicted that the most obvious point for the breakup, if containment held together long enough, would be Eastern Europe. This vision was borne out in 1989, but not before the United States had altered, militarized, and generalized containment policy far beyond the original plan. The result was a global commitment to combat communism "at any price." The cost for America and its allies was great indeed.

SEATO: Acronym for Southeast Asia Treaty Organization. Established 1954. Countries participating included: Australia, France, New Zealand, Pakistan, the Philippines, Thailand, the United Kingdom, and the United States. The objectives of the organization were to prevent and counter communist subversion and to uphold the principles of self-determination and self-government. An (unrealistic) insistence on unanimity in decision making, among other factors, led to dissolution in 1977.

Harry S Truman: 1844-1972. Thirty-third president of the US (1945-53). Truman was responsible for some of the most momentous decisions in the history of US global relations: the atomic bombing of Japanese cities; countermeasures to Soviet aggression, including the Berlin Airlift, the Truman Doctrine, the Marshall Plan, and NATO; fighting the invasion of South Korea with American and United Nations forces; and the refusing to recognize the communist government of China. All these decisions shaped American foreign policy in the post–WWII era.

Truman Doctrine: On 12 March 1947, President Harry Truman proclaimed "it must be the policy of the United States to support free peoples who are resisting attempted subjugation by armed minorities or outside pressures." Widely interpreted to have obligated the United States to resist Soviet expansionism wherever it appeared in the world, the policy implied a confrontational stance during a period in which America was demobilizing its army and radically reducing its defense expenditures. At first, the Truman Doctrine lacked a strategy for implementation, but this was soon supplied by analysts such as George Kennan in the initial formulation of "containment policy."

■ China

Chongqing: (choong ching) Located in southwest China at the junction of the Yangzi and Jialing Rivers, Chongqing is a major city in Sichuan Province and was the provisional capital of Republican China from 1938 to 1945.

Generalissimo: Chiang Kai-shek's title for himself.

■ Korea

Choson Inmin Konghwaguk: (choe son in min kohng hwah gook) Korean for Korean Peoples' Republic.

DPRK: Acronym for Democratic Peoples' Republic of Korea; commonly called North Korea.

Kim Il Sung: (kim ill soong) Born Kim Song-ju in 1912, Kim has been the sole leader of the Democratic People's Republic of Korea since its founding in September 1948. Under Kim's direction, North Korea has become isolated from the outside world, even within the Soviet bloc.

Korean War: A confrontation between the Republic of Korea (ROK), the US, and the UN on one side, and the Democratic People's Republic of Korea (DPRK), the Soviet Union, and the PRC on the other. The official dates for the war are June 25, 1950 to July 27, 1953. From the Korean point of view, however, the conflict started immediately after the end of WWII, when Korea was divided into American- and Soviet-occupied zones, and lasts to this day; the ROK never signed the armistice which ended the armed hostilities. The demilitarized zone between the Koreas is one of the most heavily armed borders in the world.

At the end of WWII, Korea was split at the thirty-eighth parallel--an artificial division imposed by outside powers. Although the UN tried to unify the peninsula and sponsored elections in 1948, the Soviets denied UN representatives access to North Korea. In June 1950, the North invaded the South, and pushed the ROK forces back to a small corner in the Southeast. The MacArthur-led forces of the South launched an offensive in September, and pushed up to the Yalu River (Amnok-kang), the border with China. The PRC, feeling threatened by the proximity of enemy armies, entered the war at this point, repulsing the forces of the South. Eventually, the North worked its way back to the thirty-eighth parallel--back to where the war started. Armistice negotiations began in mid-1951 and dragged on for two years. Approximately four million people died in a war which changed no borders.

The Korean War's greatest significance for Japan was as a catalyst for economic revival and growth. It also changed the US approach to Japan--from reform of an old enemy to reconstruction of a new ally.

KPR: Acronym for Korean Peoples' Republic, the state founded on 6 September 1945.

NKPA: Acronym for North Korean People's Army. The army which invaded South Korea in 1950.

■ Vietnam

Ngo Dinh Diem: (ngo din dee-oo) 1901-1963. The president of the Republic of Vietnam (South Vietnam) from 1956 until his assassination on 2 November 1963. Classically educated and from a Catholic family, he had served in the colonial administration under the French, but resigned in 1933, claiming that the Vietnamese could exercise no real power in the colonial government. In 1954, he became PM in the State of Vietnam. Diem forced the emperor out of the government, and proclaimed the Republic of Vietnam in 1956.

Supported by the US government, Diem's administration quashed peaceful attempts to reunify Vietnam. The nepotistic Diem regime became increasingly repressive, and the Catholic Ngos stifled the Buddhist majority. This led to the famous televised self-immolations by protesting Buddhist monks.

The November 1963 coup was implicitly sanctioned by the US, and as a result of the coup, Diem, two of his brothers, and many of his supporters, were assassinated.

NLF: Acronym for National Liberation Front, the actual (translated) name for the Viet Cong.

Nguyen Van Thieu: (win vahn tree) Born 1923. A military officer in the South Vietnam Army, Thieu participated in the coups against the Ngo brothers in 1963 and against their successor in 1964. Assuming control of Saigon as premier in 1965, Thieu was elected as the last president of the Republic of Vietnam in 1967. A former general, he was spirited from Vietnam by the US before the Fall of Saigon in April 1975. He is currently thought to be living in France with his family.

Tet Offensive: *Tet* is the Vietnamese New Year, usually in late January or early February. In February of 1968, at the time of *Tet*, the Communists launched a major assault in South Vietnam. It was hoped that this offensive would lead to a popular uprising against the South Vietnamese government. Not only was there no such uprising, but the Communists suffered heavy losses during this maneuver. However, it was a major psychological victory for the Viet Cong against America, as popular opinion turned increasingly against the war effort.

Viet Cong: Short for *Viet Nam Cong San*, or "Vietnam Communism." The term was popularly used to indicate the infamous guerrillas of the Vietnam War. The VC unrelentingly attacked American forces, and seemed to be everywhere. Due to the nature of the war, women, children, and the elderly were often part of the Viet Cong. The VC infiltrated virtually every village and even American installations in their efforts to liberate their country. In military communications, the letters "V" and "C" are called "Victor" and "Charlie;" eventually, "charlie" became a common term for the Viet Cong.

TIME-FRAME QUESTIONS

1. a. Truman dismisses MacArthur.
    b. The Chinese enter the Korean War.
    c. Jacob Malik, UN delegate from the USSR, calls for armistice.
    d. MacArthur's forces take Pyongyang.
    e. Syngman Rhee boasts that the South can take Pyongyang in three days.

2. a. Mao Zedong proclaims: "China has stood up!"
    b. Battle of Dien Bien Phu.
    c. Alger Hiss convicted of perjury.
    d. The Truman Doctrine and the Marshall Plan.
    e. The NKPA invades across the thirty-eighth parallel.

3. a. Geneva Agreement.
    b. National Liberation Front established in South Vietnam.
    c. Ngo Dinh Diem becomes president of South Vietnam.
    d. President Eisenhower calls possible Vietnamese surrender to Communism a "threat."
    e. General Association of Vietnamese Buddhists founded.

4. a. Gen. Patrick J. Hurley is US Ambassador to China.
    b. The State Department issues the White Paper on China.
    c. Mao Zedong proclaims: "China has stood up!"
    d. Gen. George C. Marshall's special mission to China.
    e. McCarthy-McCarran commissions begin hunts for the culprits who "lost" China.

5. a. The southern Viet Minh is transformed into the NLF.
    b. Nguyen Van Thieu becomes leader of Saigon government.
    c. The Viet Cong controls about two-thirds of Southern villages.
    d. Successful coup carried out by military officers against Diem.
    e. Lyndon Johnson calls Ngo Dinh Diem the "Winston Churchill" of Southeast Asia.

6. a. The Philippines become independent.
    b. George Kennan develops the theory of 'containment'.
    c. Madame Chiang Kai-shek addresses the US Congress.
    d. Patrick Hurley becomes the US Ambassador to China.
    e. The establishment of North and South Korea.

QUESTIONS FOR REVIEW

1. Look at the list of Key Concepts and Names for this chapter. Find all the place names, then locate each place on the maps in the text.

2. What was the other major non-Asian power that was aggressively influential in East Asia? How important was the US perception of that power and its influence to the development of American foreign policy initiatives? Why?

3. Where are Subic Bay and Clark Field? Why are they important to the US? What is the controversy surrounding them and how has this controversy shaped American relationships in the Pacific area?

4. Describe the international situation that formed the background to George Kennan's policy of containment. Why do you think the term "containment" was adopted for Kennan's policy? What were the differences between Kennan's original emphasis and the emphases of later presidential administrations?

5. Why was Alger Hiss important to the development of American foreign policy after WWII? What international events influenced public attitudes toward Hiss? domestic events?

6. Describe the American reaction to Mao's announcement of 1 October 1949 from Tian'anmen. Why would the US have a reaction at all?

7. The Korean War began and ended with the thirty-eighth parallel serving as the division between the North and the South. With this result in mind, how would you describe the outcome of the war? Was it a victory or a defeat for either side? What importance, if any, do you think the Korean War had in US history? in East Asian history? to international relations?

8. Describe the "domino" theory. How valid do you feel this theory was, at the time? What relation do you think this theory had to post–WWII developments in East and Southeast Asia? to developments in the world?

9. In what ways can Kim Il Sung be compared to the Yi rulers of Korea who shut their country off from the outside world?

ADDITIONAL RECOMMENDED READINGS

Fall, Bernard B. *Hell In A Very Small Place*. Philadelphia, PA: J.B. Lippincott Company, 1967.

Fitzgerald, Frances. *Fire In The Lake*. New York: Random House, 1973.

Halberstam, David. *The Best and the Brightest*. Greenwich, CT: Fawcett Publications, Inc., 1972.

Han Suyin. *The Morning Deluge*. Boston: Little, Brown and Company, 1972.

Hinton, William. *Fanshen*. New York: Random House, 1966.

Johnson, Chalmers A. *Peasant Nationalism and Communist Power*. Stanford: Stanford University Press, 1962.

Kahn, E.J., Jr. *The China Hands*. New York: The Viking Press, Penguin Books, 1975.

Kim, Ilpyong J., ed. *The Strategic Triangle*. New York: Paragon House Publishers, 1987.

Suh, Kuk-sung, et al., eds. *The Identity of the Korean People: A History of Legitimacy on the Korean Peninsula*. Seoul: Research Center for Peace and Reunification, 1983.

Tan, Amy. *The Joy Luck Club*. New York: Ballantine Books, 1989.

Tuchman, Barbara W. *Stillwell and the American Experience In China, 1911-1945*. New York: The MacMillan Company, 1971.

UNIT ELEVEN

China's Long March Toward Modernization

OVERVIEW

This unit tells the story of the PRC's effort to modernize and, in particular, the impact of Deng Xiaoping's Four Modernizations. After a long and costly succession of half-starts and failures, China's leaders must not only deal with a century and a half of neglect; they must also confront the legacy of Mao Zedong and his ruinous Cultural Revolution.

The Four Modernizations of Deng Xiaoping are not new. First proposed by Zhou Enlai in 1964, the modernizations (of industry, agriculture, science-technology, and the military) are essentially the same objectives which China's leaders have had since the Self-Strengthening Movement of the 1870s, when Li Hongzhang and others started building railroads and arsenals. However, it took the "communization" of China under Mao to establish order and to unify hundreds of millions of people, with their different languages and customs, into one country.

But Mao's later failures were as gigantic as his early successes. When China recovered from the excesses of the 10-year Cultural Revolution (1966-1976), Mao's successor, Deng, set the country on a pragmatic course, placing economics ahead of ideology. Yet the entrenched power of Deng's own communist bureaucracy has proven to be modernization's greatest enemy.

Unlike the social convulsions of the Cultural Revolution, which went on behind a curtain of isolation from foreigners, China's current drama is played out on a relatively public international stage. While Deng's policies were remarkably successful in "opening" China to the outside world, the events in Tian'anmen Square in 1989 tarnished his image and left the nature of his legacy very much in doubt.

Even in times of isolation, China has exerted a strong influence on the nations around it. But since the beginning of the 1980s, trade and investment between China and the other Pacific nations has soared to unprecedented levels. This has created a concern in some Pacific Asian countries, such as those of ASEAN, which see a strengthening Chinese economy as a competitor rather than as a customer.

Politically, Deng's China has been welcomed. A peaceful (if nationalist) China can be a force for stability in a region where its influence was once disruptive. Yet in trying to engineer an economic revolution by common consent, he and his aging cohorts face both social and political problems, for the very economic progress he champions inevitably brings with it political ferment and greater demands for political freedom.

STUDY RESOURCES

Text: Chapter 10: *China's Long March Toward Modernization*

STUDY FOCUS

After reading Chapter 10, you should have a basic understanding of the following concepts.

1. Traditionally, Chinese leadership has not tolerated public criticism; the idea of a "loyal opposition" is unknown in China.

2. Chinese leadership requires consensus among the elite, and has no institutionalized method for incorporating new interest groups.

3. In the PRC, economic modernization is paramount--democracy and political reform will be sacrificed for economic development.

4. Nationalism in the PRC is defined in cultural terms. Any "cultural impurities," such as foreign ideologies and Westernization, are seen as threats to Chinese polity.

5. As China's economy has become increasingly integrated with the world economy, the policies that have facilitated this cannot be reversed without serious economic hardship and political cost.

6. China's biggest challenge continues to be overpopulation.

7. Imbalances between coastal development, e.g., the Open Door policy and Special Economic Zones, can be contrasted to China's traditionally poor interior.

KEY CONCEPTS AND NAMES

This is a list of important terms and people that you should understand from reading the text. If you cannot think of a brief explanation for everything on this list, you need to read the text again.

Beijing Spring
Cultural Revolution
Deng Xiaoping
Four Modernizations
Gang of Four
Great Leap Forward
Hu Yaobang
Jiang Qing
Mao Zedong

Maoism
One-Child Policy
People's Liberation Army
Red Guards
Soviet Model
Tian'anmen Square/Massacre
Zhao Ziyang
Zhou Enlai

GLOSSARY

■ China

Beijing Spring: The name for the events which occurred in Beijing and were centered in Tian'anmen Square during the spring of 1989.

1989 was the seventieth anniversary of the May Fourth Movement. There were to be commemorative ceremonies in Tian'anmen Square, and students gathered in Beijing. Hu Yaobang, who had been a champion of student causes, died on 15 April 1989. His death was seen as a great loss, and students assembled in the Square to mourn his passing.

This protest quickly developed into a serious contest of wills between the central government and the students. As the time for Mikhail Gorbachev's historic state visit to the PRC approached, a visit which was to repair the 30-year-old rift between the PRC and the USSR, the ranks of protesting students had swelled to fill the square. Workers, professionals, and ordinary Beijing residents joined the students in Tian'anmen Square, bringing the number of protesters to an estimated one million. A hunger strike to underline the call for democratic reforms was begun on 13 May.

Journalists from around the world were in Beijing to document Gorbachev's visit to the PRC. However, the protesters overshadowed Gorbachev. The televised occupation of Tian'anmen Square was an embarrassment to the Chinese government.

The government was divided on how to approach the demonstration. When Party General Secretary Zhao Ziyang broke the silence and openly supported the students, before a governmental consensus had been reached, he forced the government's hand.

Premier Li Peng declared martial law on May 20, but the protesters remained in Tian'anmen Square. Soon thereafter, the PLA tried to move in, but the Army was thwarted by Beijing citizens, who blocked the advancing units. Beyond just stopping their progress, the public was able to win the support of the local PLA units.

In the pre-dawn hours of 3-4 June 1989, PLA troops from northwestern China firmly cracked down on the student protesters occupying Tian'anmen Square. Estimates of the number of unarmed civilians killed go into the thousands.

Cultural Revolution: The Great Proletarian Cultural Revolution was initially another attempt by Mao to "purify" China and to restore revolutionary righteousness. Mao went outside of the power structure and used his sizable personal prestige to motivate the masses. It was also an attempt by Mao to regain the paramount leadership he had partially forfeited as a result of the failure of the Great Leap Forward.

Although the dates are often given as 1966 to 1976, the GPCR is generally considered to have passed through three stages: 1966-69, when the Red Guards were in control and a total social disintegration threatened; 1969-71, when the PLA under Lin Biao reestablished social order, and Lin emerged as Mao's heir-apparent; and 1972-76, when both Zhou's and Mao's health deteriorated, the Gang of Four gained leadership, and the PRC increasingly turned away from global involvement. With Mao's death in 1976 and the subsequent arrest of the Gang of Four, China's "Decade of Shame" officially came to an end.

Democracy Wall: Refers to a wall near Beijing University where hundreds of "big character" posters were put up in 1978 ("big character" posters are wall-sized posters, written in oversized characters, with political content). At first, this was encouraged by the authorities as a means to criticize the Cultural Revolution and Mao Zedong. However, when this expanded beyond those simple goals and became an unofficial nationwide pro-democracy movement, the authorities cracked down on the students and their supporters. Posters criticizing the government were allowed on Democracy Wall during 1978-1979; the Democracy Wall Movement was from 1978 to 1981.

Fang Lizhi: (fahng lee jer) Chinese astrophysicist, born 1936 in Beijing. Upon entering Beijing University in 1952, he distinguished himself as an outstanding scientist and champion of freedom of inquiry and expression.

Fang was purged and expelled from the CCP during the Anti-Rightist Campaign of 1957. He was abused again during the Cultural Revolution. After the end of the Cultural Revolution and the fall of the Gang of Four, Fang was rehabilitated. He regained CCP membership and became China's youngest full professor in 1978. Soon thereafter, he became one of the few Chinese scientists of international stature.

As contacts between faculty and students and the rest of the world increased, Fang committed himself to educational reform, particularly the creation of intellectual and academic freedom.

Fang supported the students during the Beijing Spring of 1989. After the crackdown, he sought asylum at the American Embassy in Beijing; he was allowed to leave the country the following year.

Five Year Plan: A plan for economic development, designed to be implemented over a period of five years. Although usually associated with socialist countries, five year plans have also been utilized by capitalist state economies. The basic features usually include a set of five yearly quotas in agricultural and industrial production, yearly increases in these quotas, and central administration of the plan, or, at least, cooperation between the state and the production sectors of a non-socialist economy. Five year plans have been utilized for both economic and political reform, especially in China. Recently, five year plans have incorporated the promotion of international trade, particularly the development of exports.

Four Modernizations: Originally proposed by Zhou Enlai in a 1964 speech, the Four Modernizations have become the basis of the economic reform program instituted in 1978 by Deng Xiaoping. These four segments of the PRC economy have been established as the initial areas to be modernized by the year 2000: agriculture; heavy and light industry; national defense; science and technology. No matter what the subject, Deng often used the achievement of the Four Modernizations as the main theme in the majority of his speeches in the 1980s.

Gang of Four: Refers to Jiang Qing, Wang Hongwen, Yao Wenyuan, and Zhang Chunqiao. Jiang Qing was Mao's (third) wife; the other members of the Gang of Four were also close to Mao. These four were the leaders of the ultraleftist wing of the CCP during the Cultural Revolution.

At their peak, the Gang of Four purged many CCP leaders and seized power in China's propaganda, cultural, and educational structures. However, they were unable to dominate the bureaucracy, had little popular support, and no support from the military.

After Mao's death in 1976, Hua Guofeng and military leaders were able to arrest the Gang of Four. After Deng Xiaoping returned to power

132

(the Gang of Four had purged him), the Gang of Four was publicly put on trial during 1980-81. After being found guilty on a variety of charges, Jiang Qing and Zhang Chunqiao were sentenced to death; their sentences were commuted to life imprisonment. Wang Hongwen was sentenced to life; Yao Wenyuan received twenty years.

Great Leap Forward: An economic and social experiment engineered by Mao in 1957, and implemented in 1958. The Great Leap Forward came after the successes of the first Five-Year Plan. Combining elements from the Soviet model and Mao's own ideas, the Great Leap Forward stressed two points: to harness "the collective will of the people" to overcome any obstacle; and to make one "great leap" to communism, without going through any intermediate stages. Mao sought to supersede Soviet dominance of world communism and to develop a distinct "Chinese model" of communism.

The Great Leap Forward saw the collectivization of the Chinese countryside. Peasants were organized into military-style communes. Communes were required to be entirely self-sufficient. This meant that each commune had to produce its own goods, build whatever it needed on its own, and take care of its own social needs.

By the end of 1959, it was obvious that the Great Leap Forward was not working. However, it was not dismantled until 1962. Mao was blamed for the failure of his idea; he was criticized within the CCP Central Committee. Mao recognized his mistake, and in 1962, he reluctantly stepped down from daily decision making in the government and the CCP.

Hu Yaobang: (who yow bahng) 1915-1989. General Secretary of the CCP from 1981-1987 and Deng's personally selected heir-apparent. Hu developed his political base through long involvement with the Communist Youth League, which recognizes and recruits outstanding youths for grooming as CCP cadres. Hu was known as a moderate reformer who gained his position through his strong support of Deng's economic modernizations. He was also a particular champion of youth and student issues. His death was an important component of the Beijing Spring.

Jiang Qing: (jahng ching) 1914-1991. An actress in Shanghai in the 1930s, Jiang travelled to communist headquarters in Yan'an in 1937. She caught the attention of Mao, and the two soon became constant companions. Mao's second wife was sent to the USSR to recuperate, and it is thought that Mao and Jiang married soon thereafter. However, no marriage document has been located.

In 1965, Jiang formed what came to be called "The Gang of Four." Insisting that socialist ideology was the sole basis for art, the Gang dominated the Chinese cultural scene until the end of the Cultural Revolution. Arrested in 1976, Jiang was tried in 1980, found guilty, and sentenced to death. Her sentence was commuted to life imprisonment and later, house arrest. She committed suicide in 1991.

Li Peng: (lee puhng) Born 1928. Li was educated in Moscow as a hydroelectric engineer; because of this, he has had strong ties with the Soviet Union and Eastern Europe. He was instrumental in repairing Sino-Soviet relations. In 1988, he replaced Zhao Ziyang as premier, Zhao having moved up to CCP General Secretary in 1987. A conservative hard liner, Li has been an advocate of central control, state planning, and heavy industry (i.e., the Soviet model).

Lin Biao: (lynn bee-ow) 1907-1971. Born in Hubei Province, Lin graduated from the Whampoa Military Academy in Guangzhou in 1926. Upon graduation, he joined the CCP.

Lin was a military commander for the CCP. He was also a survivor of the Long March. He worked with Zhou Enlai in the CCP-KMT liaison office. Lin led CCP troops to many victories in the Chinese Civil War of 1945-49, including the capture of Beijing.

Lin was largely absent from public view until the early sixties, when he rose to vice-chairman of the Party in 1966, and was designated heir apparent to Mao. Lin was also one of the editors of Mao's infamous "little red book."

In the early 70s, there was a falling out between Mao and Lin. Amidst a conspiracy to assassinate Mao, Lin, with his wife and son, attempted to flee to the USSR. However, their plane was allegedly shot down over Mongolia on 12 September 1971; there were no survivors. Lin has been posthumously denounced on several occasions, and remains in disgrace.

Liu Shaoqi: (leo shao chee) 1898-1969. The chief theoretician of Chinese communism and the first president of the PRC. During the Cultural Revolution, Liu was purged; he died in internal exile. In 1980, Deng Xiaoping posthumously rehabilitated his old friend Liu.

Mao Zedong: (mao tsuh doong) 1893-1976. First secretary of the Chinese Communist Party (1943-1976) and the dominant leader of the People's Republic of China after its establishment in 1949. After the communist victory in the Chinese Civil War (1945-49) and his emergence as China's premier leader, Mao instituted a series of revolutionary and controversial reforms, such as the Great Leap Forward and the Cultural Revolution. The extremism of his later years has led to a reassessment of Mao and Maoist thought. Official communist evaluation of Mao is "70/30", meaning that the first 70% of his life is seen as beneficial, and the remaining 30% was detrimental. This verdict has made it possible for the more pragmatic Deng Xiaoping to implement various reforms that would have been anathema to Mao.

Maoism: A philosophy of continuous revolution based on concepts proposed by Mao Zedong. The components were: peasant leadership; rural agrarian bases; anti-intellectualism; mass movements; purges of "counter-revolutionaries;" and the destruction of social structures. Paramount to Maoism is the preeminence of the "correct" ideological orientation. Maoism stands to the left of communism and has never been successfully implemented. Ultimately, Maoism was a personality cult, fostered by Mao in his desire to retain control in post-1949 China.

PLA: Acronym for People's Liberation Army, the army of the PRC.

Red Army: Another name for the PLA. In a more general sense, the term can be applied to any communist country's army.

Red Guards: At first, Red Guards were groups of students at Beijing University and other national universities. Soon, there were Red Guard units made of secondary and primary school students, workers, and peasants on communes. Modeled on the PLA, Red Guards were a response to Mao Zedong's call for a new effort at mass revolutionary mobilization during the Cultural Revolution.

Eventually, rival Red Guard units formed within the same school, factory, or commune, each claiming to have "purer revolutionary zeal" than the other units. This quickly escalated into violence; thousands lost their lives. Various Red Guard units, in their attempts to be the "most revolutionary," were responsible for destroying countless numbers of China's cultural monuments. Anything representative of the Four Olds, and anything "Western," was a target. Temples were sacked, statues were defiled, homes were looted, and mayhem prevailed throughout the country. By late 1966, it became apparent that the Red Guards were out of control. The PLA was instructed to regain control of the country from the Red Guards in 1967. By 1969, the Red Guards ceased to be significant in China's internal politics.

Tian'anmen Massacre: (tea-en ahn mun) The tragic conclusion to the Beijing Spring of 1989. Li Peng declared martial law on 20 May, but the protesters remained in Tian'anmen Square. Soon thereafter, the PLA tried to move in, but their efforts were thwarted by students and citizens.

In the pre-dawn hours of 3-4 June 1989, PLA troops firmly cracked down on the student protesters occupying Tian'anmen Square. The troops used automatic weapons on unarmed civilians and used tanks to crush tents occupied by hunger-strikers. Although official figures for casualties are extremely low, with more PLA losses than civilian losses, outside China these figures are dismissed as mere propaganda. Within one week of the Massacre, hospitals verified more than 700 civilian deaths. Some estimates go as high as 7,000 dead, but the true figure may never be known.

The troops that carried out the Massacre were brought in from western China, as the local troops could not be enjoined to move against the students and their supporters. It remains unknown who in the leadership ordered the crackdown; the PRC still reverberates from the impact of this blow to the pro-democracy movement.

Tian'anmen Square: Located in the heart of Beijing, Tian'anmen means "Gate of Heavenly Peace." Tian'anmen Square is the largest public square in the world and serves as China's ceremonial center.

Located immediately south of the old Imperial palace, Tian'anmen Square is flanked by the Gate of Heavenly Peace to the north, another of Beijing's old city gates to the south, museums to the east, and the Great Hall of the People to the west. Within the square itself are the Monument to the People's Heroes at the center and Mao Zedong Memorial Hall in the south, where Mao's body lies in state.

Tian'anmen Square was the site of the student protests of 1905, 1911-12, 1919, 1925, and 1976; the Beijing Spring protests of 1989; and the Tian'anmen Massacre.

Yang Shangkun: (yahng shahng coon) Born 1907. President of the PRC and vice chairman of the Central Military Commission since 1987, Yang has stressed reform of the armed forces and modernization of national defense. A conservative, Yang has gained more power since the Tian'anmen Massacre.

Zhao Ziyang: (jao tsuh yahng) Born 1919. A bureaucrat and member of the CCP, Zhao was purged during the Cultural Revolution. However, he was rehabilitated and became governor of Sichuan Province in 1975. Elected to the Politburo in 1979, he became premier in 1980. Upon the death of Hu Yaobang in 1987, Zhao became the Party General Secretary. As Party General Secretary, he was heir apparent to Deng. He held this post until the Tian'anmen Massacre, after which he disappeared from public sight. Although he was sighted in China in 1990, his official status is unknown as of 1991.

136

Zhou Enlai: (joe en lie) 1898-1976. Zhou came from a scholar-gentry background, and was tutored in traditional Confucian precepts before attending modern Chinese schools in his native Tianjin. After spending some time in Japan, Zhou went to France in 1920 on the work-study program; he joined the French cell of the CCP in late 1921.

After his return to China, Zhou became the political director of the Whampoa Military Academy in Guangdong province. The commandant of Whampoa was Chiang Kai-shek, who eventually turned on Zhou and ordered his death. Zhou escaped and went underground, organizing urban laborers. When urban areas became too dangerous, Zhou escaped to Mao's mountain retreat. In 1934-35, Zhou commanded the first stage of the Long March. Zhou's support of Mao was critical to the development of the CCP along Maoist lines.

When the Second United Front of the KMT-CCP was established to fight against the Japanese, Zhou served as the CCP representative in the KMT capital of Chongqing, meeting with both KMT and American officials. When WWII ended, Zhou returned to the CCP forces and represented the CCP in subsequent futile negotiations with the KMT. When Mao proclaimed the PRC on 1 October 1949, Zhou was by his side. Zhou was the PRC's Foreign Minister, and from 1954 until his death, he was the PRC's Premier. Charming and urbane, Zhou presented the PRC's face to the diplomatic world and developed favorable relationships with many countries. Zhou staged one of the diplomatic coups of the twentieth century when he greeted President Richard Nixon on the tarmac of the Beijing airport in September 1972.

Zhou has long been regarded as the "Great Pragmatist" who put the needs of the Chinese masses above all else. An ardent nationalist, Zhou was staunchly communist and, even more strongly, a backer of Mao. In recent years, his public image within the PRC has been eroded by a re-evaluation of his apparent tacit endorsement of the excesses of the Cultural Revolution. Zhou has been called an enigma, and remains one of the least discussed of the founders of the PRC.

Zhu De: (jew duh) 1886-1976. Zhu had been trained as a soldier and served in the military for most of his life. Commanding a warlord army in the 1920s, he became convinced that communism and Mao Zedong's approach were key to China's future during the abortive Autumn uprising of 1927. He left his warlord employer and joined Mao's forces, taking with him some of his own troops. Zhu was a military adviser on the Long March, and helped to form the PLA. He was regarded as the father of the modern PRC military structure, and given the title of Marshal.

▪ Tibet

Xizang: (she tsang) Literally "Western Storehouse," Xizang is the Mandarin name for Tibet. It is the name given to Tibet by the Chinese after the Chinese invasion of 1950. It is one of the officially designated "Minority Autonomous Regions," which (in theory) makes the region self-governing. In actual practice, Tibet has been under military control since its annexation.

TIME-FRAME QUESTIONS

1. a. Great Leap Forward.
   b. Tian'anmen Massacre.
   c. Hundred Flowers.
   d. Cultural Revolution.
   e. Democracy Wall.

2. a. Death of Zhou Enlai.
   b. Death of Lin Biao.
   c. Death of Hu Yaobang.
   d. Death of Mao Zedong.
   e. Death of Josef Stalin.

3. a. Mikhail Gorbachev visits PRC.
   b. Deng Xiaoping visits Washington, DC.
   c. Ronald Reagan visits PRC.
   d. Rajiv Gandhi visits PRC.
   e. Richard Nixon visits PRC.

4. a. Dismissal of Hu Yaobang from office.
   b. Dismissal of Deng Xiaoping from office (second time).
   c. Dismissal of Zhao Ziyang from office.
   d. Dismissal of Liu Shaoqi from office.
   e. Dismissal of Peng Dehuai from office.

5. a. Sino-Indian Border Conflict.
   b. Korean War.
   c. China invades Vietnam.
   d. End of CCP-KMT civil war.
   e. Sino-Soviet Border Conflict (Ussuri River).

6. a. Soviets invade Hungary.
   b. China invades Tibet.
   c. Vietnam invades Cambodia.
   d. Revolt in Tibet.
   e. Soviets invade Czechoslovakia.

7. a. One of the greatest famines in recorded Chinese history.
   b. Arrest of the Gang of Four.
   c. Dalai Lama flees Tibet.
   d. Deng Xiaoping "rehabilitated" (second time).
   e. Beginning of Cultural Revolution.

8. a. US abrogates security treaty with Taiwan.
   b. Indonesia freezes relations with PRC.
   c. China objects to Nakasone visit to Yasukuni Shrine.
   d. US recognizes PRC.
   e. Leonid Brezhnev calls for normalization with PRC.

QUESTIONS FOR REVIEW

1. Compare and contrast the economies of China with those of the NIEs, ASEAN, and Japan. For example, examine the industrial and agricultural components of each country's economy. Confirm regional differences through map review and exercises.

2. Referring to Chapter 4, compare and contrast the Tian'anmen Massacre and the Korean March First Movement. What do these events have in common? What makes them different?

3. The Iraqi leadership justified the 1990 invasion and annexation of Kuwait by claiming that Kuwait was a "traditional" part of Iraq. What action of the PRC in 1950 parallels that event of 1990?

4. There are "Chinese" areas which are not part of the PRC. What are they? Where are they? Are there plans to incorporate any of these areas into the PRC?

5. Some of the scholars cited in Chapter 10 virtually predict the downfall of the CCP and the demise of the PRC. Why would they make such a prediction? What do you think?

6. What are the features which characterized China's economic and political policies during the 1980s? How do those features compare with the policies of the 1970s? the 1990s?

7. To which Chinese emperor has Mao Zedong been compared? Why?

8. The Chinese family has traditionally valued boys over girls. Why? How has the one-child policy affected the traditional Chinese outlook on the family? How has the one-child policy affected family itself? Has the one-child policy affected all groups in China equally?

9. Traditionally, intellectuals have been accorded the highest status in Chinese society. However, under Mao, China became strongly anti-intellectual. Intellectuals were derided as a "stinking ninth category" of counter-revolutionaries, and many intellectuals were sent to work in the fields during the Cultural Revolution. Are intellectuals treated with any more respect in post-Mao China?

10. In the Chinese view, culture defines the nation. How has this affected the CCP's propagation of its ideas of culture? How does such a view contrast with other nations' concepts of nationhood?

11. The PRC has long been averse to Western cultural influences, yet was founded on Marxist-Leninist principles. Is this contradictory? If so, why? If not, why not? Explain.

12. The average Chinese has little knowledge of the outside world. How might an "average Chinese" respond to broadcast of the Super Bowl and the World Series? What impression do you think the Chinese might have of the US after watching these sporting events and various American movies?

For reference, review your impressions of scenes from the movie "Eijanaika" in the video for Chapter 3. How did you respond to scenes of *wayang kulit* in the video for Chapter 4?

13. In the 1980s, the Chinese government brought foreign experts to China to teach a broad range of subjects, from foreign languages to economics, from the organization of religious institutions to the political process. Does this development have any historical parallels? Does this indicate a desire on the part of the Chinese leadership to Westernize China? Explain.

14. Soviet emigrés to the US often experience enormous difficulties in what we consider to be an everyday situation--shopping. After a lifetime of shortages and limited selection, many Soviets are baffled by the array of choices which confront them in the supermarket. What developments in the PRC parallel this dilemma of choice?

15. The blame for the Tian'anmen Massacre lies largely on the shoulders of Deng Xiaoping, the supreme leader of China at the time. In light of his past actions, is it surprising that he opted for suppression of the students over dialogue with them? Why or why not?

16. What are the "Four Olds?" What do they represent?

17. In its brief existence, the PRC has had enormous impact on China. In his essay, Roderick MacFarquar predicts that the communist leadership may end up like previous dynasties which were short-lived but had long-term effects on China. Why does he make this prediction? What similarities are there between the leadership of the PRC and the leadership of the dynasties he mentions? What are the differences?

ADDITIONAL RECOMMENDED READINGS

Kim, Samuel S., ed. *China and the World*. Boulder: Westview Press, 1989.

Rice, Edward E. *Mao's Way*. Berkeley: University of California Press, 1972.

Salzman, Mark. *Iron and Silk*. New York: Random House, 1986.

Snow, Edgar. *Red Star Over China*. New York: Grove/Weidenfeld, 1989.

Spence, Jonathan D. *The Search for Modern China*. New York: Norton, 1990.

Theroux, Paul. *Riding the Iron Rooster*. New York: Ballantine, 1988.

UNIT TWELVE

Section One
Beyond the Revolution: Indonesia and Vietnam

OVERVIEW

The purpose of Section One of Unit Twelve is to discuss the ways in which Vietnam and Indonesia have been the source of primary indigenous political influences over Southeast Asia since the end of World War II. Between them, they account for more than half the subregional population. Both countries trace their origins to revolutionary beginnings, but in Vietnam the struggle was far more protracted and its damaging effects more lasting. In both countries, the military has played a decisive role, but in Indonesia, once the erratic and unsuccessful policies of Sukarno had been ended, that role shifted toward a deep involvement in internal political and economic development. An emphasis on solving pressing economic issues, using market-oriented capitalist principles, continues to preoccupy Indonesia's technocrats.

In Vietnam, the senior leaders held a different perspective through the 1970s. Their economy in shambles, they continued to devote vast resources to a military presence in Cambodia which, in their view, had profoundly threatened their borders through the incursions led by Pol Pot. Yet an undercurrent of change was detectable in the streets and shops of old Saigon (today's Ho Chi Minh city) where free enterprise in various tentative forms was gradually allowed to surface again. But the parallel to the ancient limits of conquest in Indochina remains: As in the case of the ancient Khmer empire that lost its rice production base, so too was Vietnam's wealth in the Mekong Delta lost to the ravages of war, military priorities and, it is argued within parts of the Vietnamese leadership, inappropriate economics. What was once a "breadbasket" of Southeast Asia is still visibly blotched by bomb craters. It was also choked with ideologically-minded managers until a new policy of agricultural reform was firmly instituted in the 1980s. As of 1989, Vietnam was once again exporting rice, although the certainty of future export gains remained in doubt.

By 1975, relations between Beijing and Hanoi had deteriorated badly. Vietnam became convinced that the Chinese sought to use the war to leave Vietnam permanently divided while the Chinese were increasingly concerned about Vietnamese reliance on the Soviet Union. The Sino-Vietnamese war that erupted in 1979 encapsulated all the region's rivalries and enmities, past and present. China and, by implication, the United States were aligned against Vietnam and the Soviet Union. This was not a "proxy war" in which surrogates were fighting on behalf of the great powers, but linkages to the cold war were obvious to all the parties involved. Ultimately, however, the roots of the conflict lay in the complex triangle of relationships between Vietnam, Cambodia, and China.

Indonesia, like Vietnam, has become self-sufficient in rice, and similarly finds itself cautiously permitting some very limited freedoms of expression. Experts will argue over which country, at any given time, has been the more restrictive in its attitude toward human rights and independent political expression, but in fact both countries remain strongly authoritarian. Indonesia has played an important role in helping move toward a resolution of the future of Cambodia, its close communications with Vietnam having been a critical factor in that progress. That Vietnam found itself tarred by the United States with the brush of an occupying force in Cambodia still rankles its leadership. Like the rest of the world, they know well the genocide that Cambodia's Khmer Rouge visited upon its population.

STUDY RESOURCES

Text: Chapter 11: *Beyond the Revolution: Indonesia and Vietnam*

STUDY FOCUS

After reading Chapter 11, you should have a basic understanding of the following concepts.

1. Indonesia and Vietnam exert considerable political influence in Southeast Asia.

2. Both Indonesia and Vietnam have formed their foreign policies independently, valuing their independence over possible ties to the superpowers.

3. Military affairs have shaped both domestic and foreign policies of Indonesia and Vietnam.

4. The mistreatment of ethnic Chinese in both Indonesia and Vietnam has affected Sino-Indonesian and Sino-Vietnamese relations in the past.

KEY CONCEPTS AND NAMES

This is a list of important terms, people, and places that you should understand from reading the text. If you cannot think of a brief explanation for everything on this list, you need to read the text again.

Bapak
Doi Moi
GESTAPU
Mohammed Hatta
Khmer Rouge
Konfrontasi
Le Duc Tho
Masyumi
New Order
Nguyen Van Linh

Nhan Dan
NLF
North Vietnam
People's Republic of Kampuchea
Pertamina
Phnom Penh
Prince Sihanouk
Socialist Republic of Vietnam
Son Sann
South Vietnam

GLOSSARY

■ General

Laos: A landlocked Southeast Asian nation bordered by Burma and China to the north, Thailand to the west, Kampuchea to the south, and Vietnam to the east. The majority of the population is of Lao ethnic stock and practices Buddhism, but there are also many minorities, including the Kha, Meo (Hmong), and Yao. Rice is the major crop; coffee, cotton, opium, tea, timber, and tobacco are also grown. There is little manufacturing, but silk, silver products, and tin are exported.

After the French withdrew from Southeast Asia in 1954, civil war broke out in Laos. This was not resolved until the declaration of the Lao People's Democratic Republic on 2 December 1975.

■ Cambodia

Angka Leoeu: Literally, "Organization on High." The Khmer Rouge called Angka Leoeu the most important political player in Cambodia.

Democratic Kampuchea: The name of Cambodia under the Khmer Rouge, from April 1975 to January 1979. Democratic Kampuchea was one of the most oppressive and most radical governments the world has known. Isolating itself from the rest of the world, the government of Democratic Kampuchea imposed the death penalty on its "enemies." Approximately one million people were killed under this regime. Cities and towns were evacuated, education and money abolished, and the agricultural production system decimated.

Kampuchea: Name adopted by current government of Cambodia. A Southeast Asian nation bordered by Laos, Thailand, Vietnam, and the Gulf of Thailand. 85% of the population is of Khmer stock and the official language is Khmer, but like many former French colonies (including Laos and Vietnam), French is spoken by many. Kampuchea has significant populations of Chinese, Chams, and Vietnamese. Its primary resource is its agricultural wealth, and Kampuchea once exported pepper, rice, rubber, and other products. However, widespread fighting in the 1970s damaged plantations, and political unrest has kept production down.

Angkor was located in what is now Kampuchea. More recently, Kampuchea was part of French Indochina. Kampuchea gained independence in 1953 under Prince Norodom Sihanouk. Sihanouk was overthrown by Lon Nol in 1970, and this government fell in turn to the Khmer Rouge in 1975. Under the Khmer Rouge and their leader, Pol Pot, an estimated one to three million Cambodians died as a result of the evacuation of cities, the establishment of slave labor camps, and the extermination of suspected intellectuals or political opponents. In 1979, Vietnam invaded Kampuchea, ousted Pol Pot, and installed a puppet government known as the People's Republic of Kampuchea.

Three factions have been vying for power recently--namely Sihanouk's National Front, the Khmer People's National Liberation Front, and Pol Pot's Khmer Rouge. The first two groups have enjoyed the support of the US and many other countries; China backs the Khmer Rouge. After Vietnam began withdrawing its troops in 1988, negotiations began among the factions. A preliminary peace agreement was signed in November 1991.

Khmer Rouge: The murderous political faction which ruled Cambodia from April 1975 to January 1979. Headed by Pol Pot, the Khmer Rouge killed approximately one million people during its four years in power.

Although the Khmer Rouge were ousted from power, they continue to play a role in the contentious politics of Cambodia.

Lon Nol: Born 1917. President of the Khmer Republic, 1971-75. Closely allied with King Norodom Sihanouk until his participation in the coup overthrowing Prince Sihanouk in 1970. Fervent anti-communist. Ruled ineptly and sent into exile, to Hawaii, in 1975.

Phnom Penh: Capital of Cambodia since 1865.

Pol Pot: Pseudonym for Saloth Sar, leader of the Khmer Rouge.

Tuol Sleng: One of the most infamous of the Khmer Rouge's torture centers. See text (Chapter 11) for details.

■ Indonesia

East Timor: A former Portuguese colony, East Timor was invaded and unilaterally annexed by Indonesia in 1976.

GESTAPU: Indonesian acronym for the 30 September Movement of 1965 at which time an attempted coup occurred, probably led by elements of the Army, with support from the Indonesian Communist Party. The event represents a watershed in Indonesia's modern political history leading to a conservative crackdown on political opposition parties, a purging of the bureaucracy, and a reconsideration of governmental policies.

GOLKAR: See Unit Nine.

■ Vietnam

Dong: (dong) The Vietnamese unit of currency.

Hanoi: (hah noy) The capital of modern Vietnam, and also its largest city. It was in Hanoi that the establishment of the Democratic Republic of Vietnam was announced on 2 September 1945. Hanoi serves as the administrative and communications center of Vietnam. It is also the home to industry and commerce.

Indochinese Communist Party: See Unit Four.

Republic of Vietnam: Also known as South Vietnam. Founded in Saigon in 1955 under Ngo Dinh Diem as a result of the 1954 Geneva Accords. Lasted until the fall of Saigon in April 1975.

Saigon: (sigh gone) Officially known as Ho Chi Minh City. Located north of the Mekong delta, Saigon is the former capital of the now-defunct Republic of Vietnam. From 1867, it served as the capital of the French colony of Cochinchina. After the fall of the Republic of Vietnam, Saigon was renamed Ho Chi Minh City, in honor of the founder of the modern Vietnamese state. However, even with the official change of name, most Vietnamese continue to call it Saigon. Due to the long history of foreign influence, both as the French colonial capital and the American presence in South Vietnam, Saigon is Vietnam's most cosmopolitan city.

Socialist Republic of Vietnam: The official name of unified Vietnam, established in July of 1976.

TIME-FRAME QUESTIONS

1. a. Indonesian General Benny Murdani visits Hanoi.
    b. President Ford visits Jakarta.
    c. Nguyen Van Linh visits Moscow.
    d. September 30 incident (GESTAPU).
    e. GOLKAR established by Indonesian Army.

2. a. Founding of National Liberation Front.
    b. Founding of Democratic Republic of Vietnam.
    c. Founding of Socialist Republic of Vietnam.
    d. Founding of People's Republic of China.
    e. Founding of Democratic Kampuchea.

3. a. Vietnam divided into North and South.
    b. Pol Pot removed from power.
    c. Suharto's "New Order" implemented.
    d. Korea divided into North and South.
    e. Advent of "Guided Democracy."

4. a. Independence gained by Indonesia.
    b. Independence gained by Malaysia.
    c. Independence gained by Vietnam.
    d. Independence gained by Singapore.
    e. Independence gained by Brunei.

5. a. Vietnam invades Democratic Kampuchea.
    b. US troops arrive in Da Nang.
    c. Indonesia invades East Timor.
    d. PRC invades Vietnam.
    e. US invades Cambodia.

6. a. Sukarno dies.
    b. Ho Chi Minh dies.
    c. Mao dies.
    d. Park Chung-hee (Pak Chong-hui) assassinated.
    e. Ngo Dinh Diem assassinated.

QUESTIONS FOR REVIEW

1. Look at the list of Key Concepts and Names for this chapter. Find all the place names, then locate each place on the maps in the text.

2. Characterize Sino-Indonesian relationships. Refer back to Chapter 8 for more information.

3. What is the major export commodity for Indonesia? How has this affected its foreign policy? Why has it affected foreign policy? Confirm through map review and exercises.

4. What happened in Cambodia in the 1970s? What are the regional implications of such severe unrest?

5. What were the effects of the increased freedom of the press in Vietnam in the late 1980s? What does "freedom of the press" mean in a totalitarian state? Compare and contrast with the constraints on freedom of the press in other countries (e.g., Indonesia).

6. What are the problems of reform in a communist country? What specific problems have affected the PRC? Vietnam? What are the dangers of partial reform? Compare Vietnam's situation to events in the USSR in 1991 (e.g., the attempted coup).

7. Vietnam's communist leaders find it difficult to believe that businesses in capitalist nations are not a single, monolithic bloc (e.g., oil companies, banks) rather than competing businesses independent of government? How do you think this may affect their efforts to build ties to the capitalist world?

8. Who is Pol Pot? What is he the leader of? What did his power group do?

9. The modern state of Indonesia is a conglomeration of many different peoples with varied religious backgrounds and languages. How did the idea of one Indonesian nation evolve in this incredible diversity?

10. Indonesia remains heavily controlled by a network of generals. Examine current news accounts of political developments in Indonesia. Do they indicate differences within the military concerning the future directions the country should take? How might the interests of the military diverge from those of President Suharto, who is accused of having greatly enriched his relatives in the process of building his power?

ADDITIONAL RECOMMENDED READINGS

Brown, Frederick Z. *Second Chance: The United States and Indochina in the 1990s.* New York: Council on Foreign Relations Press, 1989.

Chanda, Nayan. *Brother Enemy: The War After the War.* New York: Harcourt Brace Jananovich, 1986.

Crouch, Harold. *The Army and Politics in Indonesia.* Ithaca, NY: Cornell University Press, 1988.

Duiker, William J. *Vietnam Since the Fall of Saigon.* Athens: Ohio University Press, 1985.

Emmerson, Donald K. *Indonesia's Elite: Political Culture and Cultural Politics.* Ithaca, NY: Cornell University Press, 1975.

UNIT TWELVE

Section Two
The Siberian Salient: Russia in Pacific Asia

OVERVIEW

Section Two of Unit Twelve focuses on the Soviet Far East. A tradition of Russian expansion toward and along the Pacific coast of East Asia began in seventeenth century. Defeat in the Russo-Japanese War brought only a temporary check to Russian territorial ambitions in the region, but after the Bolshevik Revolution, its efforts to exert influence there took on a different dimension. Led by dedicated ideologues and agents like Michael Borodin, first the Comintern, and after it, the increasingly nationalist politicians of Stalin's Soviet Union, tried to reestablish the political hold of Soviet Communism in East Asia. They were not notably successful. Even the most able Soviet ideologues were unable to keep their ideology free from Russian nationalist self-interest. Their ideas of Marxism-Leninism were based solely on European models and did not travel well in Asia. Mao Zedong demonstrated this in China. Other Asian communists may have taken their training in Moscow, but they tended to build their version of socialism in their own way.

At the close of World War II, history handed the Soviets a great opportunity. Comfortable late starters in the Pacific War, the Soviets were able to take over Manchuria and the northern half of Korea at virtually no cost. The Soviets systematically looted Manchuria, crating up much of its Japanese-built industry for shipment to the Soviet Union. They did not readily collaborate with their Chinese communist allies. They were notably reluctant to give up Port Arthur, seized after the war. In 1960, Nikita Khrushchev peremptorily withdrew Soviet advisors and economic support from China, precipitating a rift that nearly ended in open warfare and which has only partially healed.

Russian influence on postwar Japan was equally negative. Insistence on toeing the Moscow line strictly deprived a capably-led Japanese Communist Party of a chance to expand its base. The Soviet retention of border islands off the northern coast of Japan, along with a variety of military threats, have hardened the visceral anti-Russian feelings of the Japanese.

Why did the Soviet Union keep this negative stance for so long in its Asia-Pacific relations? Partly, it is historical memory. From the outset of World War II, the Soviets knew that had the Japanese elected to launch an offensive against them from the east, it would have been fatal to their struggle with the Germans in the west. Hence, we must approach the Soviet Far East from the standpoint of a nation that long has viewed it as a distant, vulnerable eastern flank. Well into the 1980s, Soviet policy in the Pacific seemed to be based on military threat alone, with none of the relatively subtle political and economic overtures that characterized Soviet policies toward NATO countries. Considering the possibilities and opportunities offered, the net gain for the Soviets after more that a century as a Pacific power would have to be reckoned as a minus quantity. Mikhail Gorbachev's speech in Vladivostok in 1986 may have signaled a sharp turnaround in the traditional Soviet stance towards its Asian neighbors, but the turmoil inside the Soviet Union, combined with years of inept and inadequate construction of a Far Eastern infrastructure, suggest that the Soviet (or Russian) capacity to become a significant economic player in Asia will remain limited for some time to come.

STUDY RESOURCES

Text: Chapter 12: *The Siberian Salient: Russia in Pacific Asia*

STUDY FOCUS

After reading Chapter 12, you should have a basic understanding of the following concepts.

1. The Soviet Far East has considerable but underdeveloped natural resources.

2. The Soviet Far East has a long history of independence from the center of Russia/the Soviet Union.

3. The regionalist tendencies of the Soviet Far East reflect the kind of fragmentation taking place elsewhere in the Soviet Union, but are unlikely to divide the Russian republic.

4. There is a long history of territorial conflict in the Northern Pacific region, as represented today by border conflicts with China and Japan. Confirm through map review.

KEY CONCEPTS AND NAMES

This is a list of important terms, people, and places that you should understand from reading the text. If you cannot think of a brief explanation for everything on this list, you need to read the text again.

Alaska
Aleutians
Amur River
Bering Straits
Far Eastern Republic
Glasnost
KGB
Kuriles
Lake Baikal
Manchuria

Maritime Region
Northern Territories
Perestroika
St. Petersberg
Sakhalin
Siberia
Soviet Far East
Stalin/Stalinism
Ussuri River
Vladivostok

GLOSSARY

■ General

Amur River: Called Heilongjiang in Mandarin Chinese, this river forms part of the eastern boundary between the Soviet Union and the PRC. There have been several border conflicts between the USSR and PRC over the Amur River.

Bering Strait: The Bering Strait divides Alaska and the (Soviet) Chukotskiy peninsula; it also connects the Bering Sea and the Chukchi Sea.

Kurile Islands: An arc of islands stretching from Hokkaido to Kamchatka. The Kuriles mark the boundary between the Sea of Okhotsk and the Pacific Ocean. Also spelled Kuril. Legitimate possession of the southernmost Kuriles is disputed by Japan and the Soviet Union.

Northern Territories: Translation of the Japanese term for the formerly Japanese islands seized by the Soviet Union at the end of WWII. Although Japan once controlled the entire Kurile chain and the southern half of Sakhalin, the Japanese government presently claims only Etorofu, Kunashiri, Shikotan, and the Habomai group. As the Soviets have not returned the islands, the Japanese refuse to sign a treaty formally ending WWII.

Sakhalin: An island in the Sea of Okhotsk. Japan won the southern half of Sakhalin as spoils of the Russo-Japanese War (see Chapter 3). The Soviets recaptured southern Sakhalin in the final days of WWII.

Ural Mountains: A mountain range in the Soviet Union, the Urals mark the traditional boundary between Asia and Europe.

Ussuri River: A river which runs from Khabarovsk to Lake Khanka, it forms part of the easternmost boundary between the PRC and the USSR.

▪ Russia/Soviet Union

Apparatchik: Russian for "bureaucrat." *Apparatchiki* serve in the Soviet and communist bureaucracy.

Lake Baikal: A vast lake north of Mongolia in the southeastern part of the Soviet Union. It is the deepest non-oceanic body of water on Earth, and contains about one-fifth of the fresh water on the surface of the Earth.

Bolshevik: From Russian for "majority." A term created by Lenin for his (minority) faction of Social Democrats. This faction was tightly organized along military lines, and led by a vanguard of elite intellectuals favoring violent social revolution.

Cossack: Slavic peasant warriors known for their horsemanship. Cossacks fought against the Bolsheviks in the Russian Civil War.

Glasnost: Russian for "openness." Refers to greater freedom in the USSR as a result of the reforms instituted by Mikhail Gorbachev.

October Revolution: The Russian communist revolution of October 1917. This revolution superseded the moderate, republican revolution of February 1917. The ensuing Russian Civil War lasted from 1918 to 1922.

Perestroika: Russian for "restructuring." Refers to economic and political reforms instituted by Mikhail Gorbachev.

Red Russian: A term for the Bolshevik military forces; so named for the red star they wore. The Soviet Army developed from these troops.

St. Petersberg: Located on the Gulf of Finland in the Baltic Sea, St. Petersberg was the capital of Imperial Russia. It was renamed "Leningrad" after Lenin's death in 1924; in 1991 the citizenry rejected Leningrad in favor of St. Petersberg, a decision symbolizing the demise of communism in the Soviet Union.

White Russian: Originally Czarist loyalists, White Russian came to refer to all Russians who fought against the Bolsheviks in the Russian Civil War.

TIME-FRAME QUESTIONS

1. a. Russo-Japanese War ends
   b. US Civil War ends
   c. First Sino-Japanese War ends
   d. Chinese Civil War ends
   e. Russian Civil War ends

2. a. Russian-American Company granted fur trading monopoly
   b. Commodore Perry opens Japan
   c. First Opium War ends
   d. Boxer Rebellion quelled
   e. US purchases Alaska

3. a. Sino-Soviet clash over Ussuri River border
   b. Outbreak of Korean War
   c. Soviet invasion of Afghanistan
   d. Soviet forces invade Northern Territories
   e. Establishment of Manchukuo

4. a. October Revolution
   b. May Fourth Movement
   c. Russo-Japanese military alliance
   d. Lenin dies
   e. Woodrow Wilson sends expeditionary force to Siberia

5. a. Downing of KAL Flight 007
   b. Gorbachev delivers Vladivostok Initiative
   c. Gorbachev visits South Korea
   d. Gorbachev visits Beijing
   e. US normalizes relations with PRC

6. a. US sends troops to Vietnam
   b. Soviets return Manchurian concessions to China
   c. China invades Vietnam
   d. Kwangju Massacre
   e. Tian'anmen Massacre

154

7. a. Meiji Restoration
    b. Russians expelled from Amur Valley by Manchus
    c. Russians establish Pacific naval facility
    d. Tartars burn Moscow
    e. Incorporation of the Maritime Region into the Russian empire

QUESTIONS FOR REVIEW

1. Describe the factors that have hindered Soviet development of a Pacific-Asian presence. How has the Soviet state tried to overcome these barriers? Which of these barriers are inherent and impossible to surmount?

2. What was the FER? Delineate its boundaries. Why was it created? Characterize relations between the FER and Moscow. What happened to the FER? Why?

3. Describe pre-Cold War relations between the US and Russia/the USSR. How have relations changed? What caused these changes?

4. Where are the Northern Territories? What are they? What is their significance to Pacific relations?

5. Compare and contrast US and Russian/Soviet development of their respective Pacific interests.

6. What role did the Soviet Far East play in the Russian Civil War (1918-1922)? What Pacific powers participated in this war? What role did those powers have?

7. What errors have the Soviets made in their relations with their Asian neighbors? What effect have these blunders had on international relations?

8. What are the Soviet views of the historical relationship between Russia/USSR and Japan? What are the Japanese views? How has this relationship affected the Asia-Pacific region?

9. Many voices in the Soviet Far East call for the reestablishment of an independent Far Eastern Republic. How viable would such a state be? What problems would it face in the "new world order"? How does this clash with Russian prerogatives in the Soviet Far East?

10. Characterize Russo-Japanese relations before WWII. What happened in the course of the war to dramatically alter the path of Russo-Japanese relations? What are the repercussions of this postwar shift in mutual attitudes?

11. What effect has the enormous distance between the Soviet Far East and the central authorities of Russia/the USSR had on developments in the Soviet Far East?

ADDITIONAL RECOMMENDED READINGS

Gorbachev, Mikhail. *Perestroika: New Thinking for Our Country and the World.* New York: Harper & Row, 1987.

Hosking, Geoffrey. *The Awakening of the Soviet Union.* Cambridge: Harvard University Press, 1990.

Segal, Gerald. *The Soviet Union and the Pacific.* London: Unwin Hyman, 1990.

Smith, Hedrick. *The New Russians.* New York: Random House, 1990.

Threadgold, Donald W. *Twentieth-Century Russia.* Boulder: Westview Press, 1989.

UNIT THIRTEEN

Pacific Century: The Regional Perspective

OVERVIEW

At the beginning of the Pacific Century, Asian economies were buffeted by a flood of imported goods and new technologies from the West. By the end of the century, several of those same Asian economies were producing and innovating at the leading edge of key technologies and were viewed by Westerners as a serious "threat" to their industries. Such a dramatic turnaround would have been unlikely in a region where commercial revolutions had no historic precedent. Pacific Asia, as noted in Units One and Two, had undergone previous surges in international commerce and had shown a capacity for sophisticated learning and technical advancement in earlier periods that far exceeded the levels found in the West at the same time.

Stability and growth in the Pacific Basin economy now strongly depends on the global economy, but its primary centers are Japan and the United States. It is a highly interdependent region where most of the smaller trading nations conduct more than half their trade with other states in the region. Units Six and Seven are vital for understanding the strategies that have brought about this economic transformation, but Units Four, Five, and Eight are necessary to comprehend its political paradoxes. In the broadest sense, Japan has led the Pacific economic revival and is now the dominant economic power in Asia, but its political influence is tempered by its record in the Pacific War. The prevailing political force is nationalism which forged new nations in the mid-twentieth century.

Regional cooperation remains tentative but is growing. It is unlikely to achieve the levels found in Western Europe any time soon, and the objectives of such cooperation in the Pacific Basin will remain different from those of Europe as long as the global economy remains relatively open. The role of the United States is important in this regard, for unlike Japan, which now dominates Asia economically, the United States exerts its regional influence as the preeminent global economic and military power. Its global strategy to maintain an open world economy includes leadership in regional political and economic organizations, an activity that some have suggested may contradict its global strategy.

Pacific Asia is gradually losing its stereotypical image in the West as merely a "crowded and impoverished" region, but the challenges of population, poverty, urbanization, and environmental degradation loom larger than ever for many of its societies.

STUDY RESOURCES

Video: "The Pacific Century: The Future of the Pacific Basin"
Text: Chapter 13: *Pacific Century: The Regional Perspective*

STUDY FOCUS

After viewing the video and reading Chapter 13, you should have a basic understanding of the following concepts.

1. The development of commerce in the Pacific and Asia since the nineteenth century can be contrasted to previous ages of commerce in terms of scope, scale, and identification of geographic epicenters; whereas the "locomotives" of commercial development historically were China and India, today they are Japan and the United States.

2. Asian postwar growth has relied heavily on exports to regional markets; export-led growth strategies have been aimed in particular at the United States. This trans-Pacific asymmetry in trade became a dominant feature by the 1980s, straining relationships, especially with Japan.

3. The Plaza Accord of 1985 led to the decision to allow the yen to appreciate relative to the dollar. Although this decision did not resolve trade imbalances in the Pacific, it did lead to a 50 percent reduction, in dollar terms, of America's global trade deficit. Concurrently, it had the effect of nearly *doubling* the Japanese domestic asset base.

4. During the 1980s, Japan decisively supplanted the US as the leading source of manufactured goods, new business investment, technology, and economic aid in an area stretching from South Asia to the Pacific islands. This pattern of growth was stimulated by international economic factors stemming from rising production costs in the Japanese market, leading to the location of new production off-shore.

5. In most of Pacific Asia, economic strength takes on greater or as high a priority as military capacity. The Gulf War notwithstanding, this means that Japan is a Pacific regional power whose influence has begun to eclipse the United States.

6. Pacific Basin regionalism is as yet a vaguely formed concept and the prospect of a Pacific Community, similar in scope to the European Community, is far from reality. Even so, the growth of trans-Pacific trade, which exceeded trans-Atlantic trade beginning in the early 1980s, will have a profound effect, politically, economically, and culturally, on the interaction of rimland and basin countries of the Pacific. The US has a critical role to play as the only economic superpower that can act as an intermediary between Europe and Asia.

7. Throughout Pacific Asia there is growing recognition of the extent to which underlying changes in demography, technology, and the environment in one geographical area can have a major impact in another. The implications of interdependence--in terms of resource management, population growth, migration, technology transfer, growing levels of urbanization, and environmental degradation--will have a profound affect on the future prospects of the Pacific Basin.

KEY CONCEPTS AND NAMES

This is a list of important terms, people, and places that you should understand from reading the text. If you cannot think of a brief explanation for everything on this list, you need to read the text again.

ADB
APEC
AsiaSat
Bretton Woods
Comparative Advantage
Current Account
Deficits
EAEG
European Community
"Europessimism"
"Flying Geese"
Foreign Workers
GATT
Guangdong
IMF
Life Expectancy
Minamata

Multinationals
Mutual Security Treaty
NAFTA
NIEs
ODA
Offshore Production
Oil Price Shock
PAFTAD
PBEC
PECC
Plaza Accord
Trade Imbalances
Trade Surplus
Tropical Forests
World Bank
Yen Bloc

GLOSSARY

■ General

Region: A basic unit of geographic study, a region can be defined as an area distinguished by a set of uniform characteristics. The criteria used to define regions can be physical, human, or both. Selection, mapping, and delimitation of the boundary of the geographic facts under investigation are combined in the determination of a region. Comparative study of regions helps to clarify how areas are similar, or how they differ, across the face of the globe.

The Pacific Basin has come to be described as a region both in physical terms, e.g., the Pacific Ocean, and in economic terms, e.g., the trade relationships which link selected countries across the Pacific. ASEAN is often used as an example of an organization which promotes regionalism within the Southeast Asian area of the Pacific, that is, the identification of transnational issues to be remedied through cooperation and collaboration between selected countries.

■ **Selected Pacific Basin Institutions**

Asian Development Bank (ADB): Organized in 1965, the purpose of the ADB is to promote and finance regional investment by the Economic and Social Commission for Asia and the Pacific of the United Nations (ESCAP). Interest rates are flexible and set separately for each loan. Japan and the United States are the major capital contributors; the president is ordinarily Japanese.

Pacific Trade and Development Conference (PAFTAD): Promotes policy-oriented, academic research and discussion of economic issues in the Pacific area. Originally organized in 1968, by the Japanese Foreign Ministry, the Conference has developed a series of meetings focusing on the prospects for regional trade liberalization. Because the Conference is a private organization, it has no direct impact on policy formulation.

Pacific Basin Economic Council (PBEC): Organized in 1967, PBEC's purpose is to strengthen trans-Pacific business and economic relations through expansion of trade and investment. Meets annually. A private, business-based organization.

Pacific Economic Cooperation Conference (PECC): Convener, since 1980, of government, business, and institutional leaders for the purpose of examining key regional economic growth issues in the Pacific, particularly the need to facilitate regional cooperation in specific economic sectors. PBEC and PAFTAD are represented in Standing Committee and Coordinating Group meetings. Does not act on behalf of governments in the region, but benefits from the financial support and structured participation of governments.

South Pacific Commission (SPC): Established in 1947, the Commission's purpose is to promote the social and economic welfare and advancement of the South Pacific region.

South Pacific Forum (SPF): Established in 1971, the Forum facilitates cooperation on such issues as: trade, transportation, tourism, and economic development.

QUESTIONS FOR REVIEW

1. Look at the list of Key Concepts and Names for this chapter. Find all the place names, then locate each place on the maps in the text.

2. What is the potential for a trade bloc in Asia? What are the incentives for creating one? What are the disincentives? Should Americans be concerned about the creation of an Asian trade bloc?

Should Asians be concerned about the creation of a North American trade bloc?

3. Should the Pacific Basin nations try to cooperate as a bloc to improve their competitive positions against the European Community? What factors prevent the Pacific from organizing itself in a manner similar to Europe?

4. If you could design the ingredients for a trading body in the Pacific region, what countries would you include? Explain your reasons for including some and excluding others. What benefits would you see for the average consumer in the countries you have included? What disadvantages?

5. Assume you are a senior economic planner for an Asian developing country, such as Thailand or Malaysia, that has abundant opportunities for rapid growth. What arguments might you make for placing low on your list of development priorities the solution of environmental problems? Alternatively, why might you argue the opposite point of view?

6. How vital is telecommunications for economic development? How would you rate it alongside priorities such as transportation and the environment? What aspects of telecommunications are most important?

7. What are the positive aspects of Japan's postwar role in Pacific Asia? Should Southeast Asian countries be concerned about the Japanese economic role in their economies? What diplomatic role should it try to play in the region?

8. How have changes in Japan's economic status not been matched by changes in its status vis-a-vis the United States in Pacific Asia? What aspects of the Japan-United States relationship seem most likely to be undergoing fundamental change in the 1990s?

9. Think back to the introduction to the Study Guide. Recall the section on developing a geographical perspective, particularly the concepts of site, situation, and interdependency as illustrated by international trade of natural resources and their conversion to finished products. Confirm through map review and exercises your understanding of the Pacific Asia and the Pacific Basin as distinct economic regions.

162

ADDITIONAL RECOMMENDED READING

Alves, Dora, ed. *Evolving Pacific Basin Strategies*. Washington: National Defense University Press, 1990.

Craven, John P. *The Management of Pacific Marine Resources: Present Problems and Future Trends*. Boulder: Westview Press, 1982.

Borgese, Elisabeth M., Norton Ginsburg, and Joseph R. Morgan, eds. *Ocean Yearbook*. Chicago, IL: University of Chicago Press, Annual.

Kim, Roy and Robert T. Kudrle. *The Industrial Future of the Pacific Basin*. Boulder: Westview Press, 1984.

Kotkin, Joel and Yoriko Kishimoto. *The Third Century: America's Resurgence in the Asian Era*. New York: Ballantine Books, 1988.

McCord, William. *The Dawn of the Pacific Century: Implications for Three Worlds of Development*. New Brunswick, NJ: Transaction, 1991.

Rostow, W.W. *The United States and the Regional Organization of Asia and the Pacific, 1965-1985*. Austin, TX: University of Texas Press, 1986.

Scalapino, Robert A. *The Politics of Development: Perspectives on Twentieth Century Asia*. Cambridge: Harvard University Press, 1989.

Schuh, Edward G. and Jennifer McCoy, eds. *Food, Agriculture, and Development in the Pacific Basin: Prospects for International Collaboration in a Dynamic Economy*. Boulder: Westview Press, 1986.

Segal, Gerald. *Rethinking the Pacific*. New York: Clarendon Press, 1990.

Shibusawa, Masahide, Zakaria Haji Ahmad, and Brian Bridges, *Pacific Asia in the 1990s*. London: Routledge, for the Royal Institute of International Affairs, 1992.

ANSWER KEY TO TIME-FRAME QUESTIONS

■ Unit One

1.	adebc	2.	ecabd	3.	adbec	4.	cbdea	5.	cbead
6.	bcade	7.	acdbe	8.	dcbae	9.	cabed	10.	baedc

■ Unit Two

1.	caebd	2.	dceba	3.	edbac	4.	adbec	5.	eabcd
6.	debca	7.	bdcae	8.	decab	9.	bdace		

■ Unit Three

1.	dcaeb	2.	ebdca	3.	cbead	4.	dcabe	5.	ecbad

■ Unit Four

1.	ecdab	2.	bdcae	3.	badce	4.	debac	5.	decab

■ Unit Five

1.	baecd	2.	ecadb	3.	edcba	4.	dcabe	5.	cdeba
6.	dabce	7.	ceadb	8.	edbac				

■ Unit Six

No Time-Frame Questions for this Unit

■ Unit Seven

1.	bdeca	2.	cabde	3.	ecbad	4.	adbec

■ Unit Eight

No Time-Frame Questions for this Unit

■ Unit Nine

1.	adebc	2.	cabed	3.	acedb	4.	ecbad	5.	bceda
6.	dcbea								

■ Unit Ten

1. edbac   2. daceb   3. edacb   4. adbce   5. aecdb
6. cdabe

■ Unit Eleven

1. cadeb   2. ebadc   3. ebcda   4. edbac   5. dbaec
6. badec   7. caebd   8. bdaec

■ Unit Twelve, Section One

1. debac   2. bdaec   3. daecb   4. acbde   5. becad
6. ebacd

■ Unit Twelve, Section Two

1. bcaed   2. acbed   3. edbac   4. caebd   5. eabdc
6. bacde   7. dbcea

■ Unit Thirteen

No Time-Frame Questions for this Unit

Index